# ALAS! POOR HESLOP

## The Last Fatal Duel in Wales

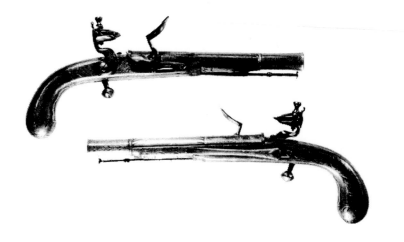

# Ken Jones

# Frontispiece

*Comment by the Judges of the King's Bench during the trial of the Athoes of Tenby in 1723.*

'It was very difficult to have justice done in Wales, for they are all related to one another, and therefore would rather acquit a criminal than have the scandal that one of their name or relations should be hanged; and that to try a man for murder in Wales was like trying to hang a man in Scotland for high treason, those being crimes not much regarded in their respective places.'

From *The Guide to the Records of the Great Sessions by Glyn Parry*, NLW 1995.

Published and printed September 2007


ISBN 978 0 9556625 0 8

Printed by E. L. Jones Argraffwyr / Printers
25 Heol y Gogledd, Cardigan. 01239 612251

*For*
*Kayleigh Amber*

# Acknowledgements

I would like to thank the following for their assistance and encouragement during the writing of this book:

My wife Ruth for her patience while I researched material for this book and for checking my grammar and spelling. To my daughter Lynne for the Cover design.

The Staff at the National Library of Wales, Aberystwyth, especially the Staff of the Reading Rooms for their grateful assistance. Glyn Parry of the NLW and Richard Ireland, University College of Wales, Aberystwyth, for their advice.

The Staff of the Royal Commission on the Ancient and Historical Monuments of Wales at Aberystwyth.

The Staff at the Ceredigion Archives at Aberystwyth and the Staff of the Carmarthenshire Archives at Carmarthen for their help. Also the Staff at the Pembrokeshire Library in Haverfordwest.

Richard Crowe for writing the chapter on Surgeon John Williams and Edward Pridham, their families and 'The Bullet.' Dr. Charles and Mary-Rose Morris for allowing me to photograph 'The Bullet' at their home in Oxfordshire.

Brawdy Books, Publishers of the Frances Jones books on Historic Homes and their Familes. The Carmarthenshire Antiquarian Society. The Proceedings of the Old Bailey Online (www.oldbaileyonline.org). The Cambrian Index Online.

Leslie Baker-Jones, Author of books on the Local Gentry for his advice and encouragement. The Rev. Towyn Jones, Carmarthen, President of the Carmarthenshire Antiquarian Society, for his help and encouragement and for writing the Foreword for this book.

The Rev. Dewi Roberts for his encouragement and allowing me to photograph Church registers. Llandilo Church for allowing me to photograph Rev. John Griffiths' memorial. Aeron Davies for his assistance at Llangeler Church. Finally, Raymond Jones for unearthing some obscure references and prints, and Alan Owen for finding *A Guide to the Collection of Welsh Bygones* by Iorwerth C. Peate (1929) and to Dylan Jones, Collections Manager St Fagans National History Museum for his assistance.

Thanks also to E. L. Jones & Son, Printers, Cardigan, for their helpful advice.

# Contents

# List of Illustrations

# Foreword

## The Reverend J. Towyn Jones
### President of the Carmarthenshire Antiquarian Society
### (Formed 1905)

'Here in the shadow of this ancient keep...' – with such words so often began the introduction by those beloved Gainsborough Films to places like Newcastle Emlyn. Somewhere long since slumbering by a lazy river but once the scene, as we were soon given to understand, of much derring-do and bloodshed. Half a century has gone by since such revelations and meanwhile tales, once popular, have been all but forgotten. Grandparents these days hardly ever have the opportunity to convey to a future generation what was handed down to them.

Not that it was always accurate by any means. On the other hand one should on no account dismiss and denigrate oral tradition. It often conveys a valuable truth which needs to be thoroughly investigated by a competent historian. Someone dedicated to the task of leaving no stone unturned. This present volume by Ken Jones admirably illustrates the point.

Apart from *Hanes Castell Newydd Emlyn* (1860) by the Reverend Benjamin Williams ('Gwynionydd' 1821-1891) and *The Story of Newcastle Emlyn and Adpar to 1531* by the Reverend Gruffydd Evans (1866-1930), the annals of Newcastle Emlyn have been largely neglected. It is to be hoped that with this excellent essay the author has only begun to redress the unfortunate situation regarding his home town.

I await with much anticipation, studies of local mysteries which have intrigued me since childhood. What is the truth regarding the fiery dragon which, according to my grandmother, descended on the castle in days of yore causing such terror in the town?

Was there truly, a sword (afterwards known as 'Cledd Cromwell') awarded to some local hero for assassinating an officer at the castle during the Civil War in the mistaken belief that it was Oliver Cromwell who, subsequently, engineered the murder of the King?

Could it possibly be so that the very bullet involved in the last fatal duel in Wales is extant? Ah! but I am about to learn the truth regarding that because that colourful drama (not to say melodrama!) is about to be revealed in exquisite detail by a very competent historian.

Little did I think as a small boy, when some of my treasured possessions (and I have them still to this day) were hand-me-down *Beano* and *Radio Fun Annuals* well thumbed by the original owner that one day I would be highly privileged to write this foreword to a book written by my benefactor for he was none other than Ken Jones.

I shall treasure this valuable contribution to the history of Newcastle Emlyn as I have treasured those other volumes from long ago. We are all in the author's debt.

# Chapter 1

# An Introduction to Duelling

It is not my intention to produce a history of duelling in this book though many different duels are mentioned, for their interest, and especially if parallels can be drawn with the *Last Fatal Duel in Wales*.

The following famous duel[1] is included because it set a bad example for the country and made out it was not disreputable to fight a duel. It was fought in 1765 between Lord Byron and Mr Chaworth. The dispute, over which of the two had the largest quantity of game on his estates, arose at a club dinner. Infuriated by wine and passion, they retired instantly into an adjoining room, and fought with swords across a table, by the feeble glimmer of a tallow-candle. Mr Chaworth, who was the more expert swordsman of the two, received a mortal wound, and shortly afterwards expired. Lord Byron was brought to trial for the murder before the House of Lords; and it appeared clearly, that the duel was not premeditated, but fought at once, and in the heat of passion. He was found guilty of manslaughter only, and ordered to be discharged on payment of his fees.

Despite this ruling duelling was still illegal and until I started this research I did not realise how popular this illegal 'sport' had been amongst the 'Gentry' with swords and pistols. With this background knowledge and the information gleaned from documents found in the local archives I hope to tell the true story of the *Last Fatal Duel in Wales*, at last.

If a 'Gentleman' was insulted or his honour was, or believed to be at stake, he would resort to sending a 'challenge,' which if accepted (it invariably was or 'lose face' and be branded a coward) ended as a duel and this had always been recognised as a way of settling matters.

A pair of duelling pistols on the wall of a country gentleman's home was thought of as a status symbol. These pistols were frequently displayed or carried in polished wooden cases in pairs. In some duels both weapons were used in turn depending on the agreement between the combatants.

---

1  *Memoirs of Extraordinary Popular Delusions and the Madness of Crowds,* Charles Mackay, 1852

The pistols were usually of the Flintlock type. These pistols had a delay between pulling the trigger and firing the bullet. Flintlock is the general term for any firearm based on the flintlock mechanism. A cock or striker tightly holding a shaped bit of flint is rotated to half-cock; the flash pan is primed with a small amount of very finely ground gunpowder, and the flashpan lid or 'frizzen' is closed. The gun is now in a 'primed and ready' state. A safety notch at half-cock prevents the hammer from falling by pulling the trigger.

To fire, the cock or striker is moved from half-cock to full-cock; the gun is aimed and the trigger pulled, releasing the striker holding the flint which strikes the hardened steel face of the frizzen, knocking the frizzen forward to uncover the small pan of gunpowder beneath it. The resulting spark ignites the powder in the pan. This flame is transferred through a small hole to ignite the main powder charge inside the barrel. This has been loaded from the muzzle end followed by shot or round lead ball, usually wrapped in a cloth or paper patch. All are rammed down with a special rod, located on the underside of the barrel. These pistols gave many new expressions to the English language, like 'flash in the pan,' 'lock, stock and barrel' and 'going off at half-cock.'

There were many duels recorded in Wales, thanks to papers like *The Cambrian*. Probably many more went unrecorded.

Our duel, 'The Last Fatal Duel in Wales,' which was never reported in the newspapers, took place in 1814 in Cardiganshire [now Ceredigion]. It happened in a dingle, just off the Cardigan Trust's turnpike [now A475] from Cardigan to Lampeter, between Adpar and Llandyfriog, about a mile from the town of Newcastle Emlyn. Newcastle Emlyn is in Carmarthenshire and is joined to Adpar in Cardiganshire by a bridge over the River Teifi.

Travellers[2] through Cardiganshire in the nineteenth century described it as a 'bare country' with land open and unenclosed. They described uncomfortable and dangerous journeys over desolate hills and the happy relief of reaching cultivated valleys like the Teifi valley, with its abundance of new mansion houses and tree plantations dotting the landscape. This was true also for the Carmarthenshire side of the river, reflecting the affluence of the local gentry whose wealth came from their landed estates.

2    *Princelings, Privilege and Power*, L. Baker-Jones, Gomer 1999, pg 61

Many were hunting people, some with their own packs of hounds. Shooting parties in season were one highlight of a squire's year.

Several of the squires often combined a profession with the rank of landowner, like attorney John Beynon of Adpar Hill or surgeon William Williams of Blaendyffryn.

It is interesting to read accounts of the area before and after the time of the duel. In 1684, Henry Somerset, the first Duke of Beaufort, had been appointed Lord President of Wales by Charles II and was Lord Lieutenant of Haverfordwest. He visited Newcastle Emlyn with Thomas Denley who kept the travel log. His report goes like this;

'That the vulgar here are most miserable and low, as the rich are happy and high both to an extreme. The 'poors' [sic] sort for bread, eat oaten cakes and drink beer (small) made of oaten malt; some drink only water from necessity.

Those of estates have their tables well spread, French wines (Claret especially), plenty and good at the rate of £5 per hogshead [46 gallons], I was informed.

They have choice wines of their own growth of the mountains, which the Welsh gentlewomen make of raspberries, which abound in these parts. The celebrated liquor here is Punch, which they make to a miracle.'

Travelling in 1796,[3] the Rev. James Burgess, Jnr., and William Williams, having walked seven miles from Llechryd, describe Newcastle Emlyn, as a 'miserable village' and were less than enamoured with their night's accommodation at a local hostelry, 'the best the town affords.'

The earliest Trade Directory found, dated 1830, by Pigot & Co. describes Newcastle-in-Emlyn as a delightful market hamlet on the River Teifi which meanders around its ancient castle, the *"Novum Castres de Emelyn"*, the 'New Castle of Emlyn,' that has given the town its name. It says that the town is fairly modern, the ancient town being the old Borough of Adpar, a borough by prescription that returned a Member of Parliament until 1742.

There were many ale-houses and hostelries on both sides of the river with ample food and clothes shops to satisfy the needs of the local

3    See Appendix 8, & J.B. Jnr and W.W. (National Library of Wales Manuscript 23253 C)

clergyman. His Church was Capel Bach y Drindod or Little Chapel of the Trinity, a chapel of ease under Kennarth [Cenarth]. It was built on the site of a medieval chapel just outside the castle gates. There are references to this chapel in 1552 and a Holy Trinity chapel in 1772.

Adpar had its own motte and bailey castle overlooking the bridge, and was also the site of the First Printing Press in Wales set up by Isaac Carter in 1718. Adpar was on the Cardigan Trust Turnpike and its Toll Houses had several visits from 'Rebecca' in the early 1840's.

Adpar or Atpar or Trehedyn, to give its old name, was a borough and township in the parish of Llandyfriog in the upper hundred of Troedyraur.

Newcastle-in-Emlyn was in the parish of Kennarth until Holy Trinity Church was built in 1842 and elevated to the dignity of a Parish Church in 1843. This incorporated the town of Newcastle Emlyn and parts of the old parish of Kennarth together with Adpar and some of the parish of lower Llandyfriog into the new parish of Newcastle-in-Emlyn.

# Chapter 2

## Duelling in General

A duel was an agreed fight, to settle differences, between two gentlemen with matched deadly weapons.

Although illegal, duelling had reached a high as a 'sport of gentlemen,' and 'gentlewomen,' especially in the late 1700's. Duels were fought in all corners of the civilised world and were very prevalent among commissioned officers in the Army and Navy. Newspapers of the time reported duels from America, Ireland, Turkey, Spain, France, India, Jamaica and Great Britain.

'Gentlewomen' fought 'petticoat duels'[4] with various types of swords. Actresses challenged one another over graceless conduct on stage; two ladies fought because of the pecking order at a society soiree. The first female duel to take place in England in 1792 was between Lady Almeria Braddock and Mrs. Elphinstone, first with a pistol when Lady A.'s hat was damaged, then with smallswords when Mrs. E. received a wound to her arm, and agreed to write an apology. This was all to do with Mrs. E. casting aspersions about Lady A.'s age.

In August 1892, in Liechtenstein, Princess Pauline Metternich and the Countess Kielmansegg met for what has gone down in history as the first 'emancipated duel' because all parties involved, including the principals and their seconds, were female. The two ladies fought topless and this was presided over by the Baroness Lubinska who kept the male servants at bay with her umbrella. The Princess drew first blood and was declared the winner. All this because of a disagreement over the floral arrangements at a forthcoming musical exhibition.

The outcome of duels varied enormously as did the 'rules' or 'Codes Duello' which governed one to one combat. Different countries had different rules, but a set of rules agreed at the Clonmel Summer Assizes in 1777 known as the 'Irish Code Duello,' was generally adopted throughout Ireland and was also favoured in America.

This duelling code was similar to the code of renaissance France and started with the 'challenger' issuing a traditional, public, personal

---

4   *Memoirs of Extraordinary Popular Delusions and the Madness of Crowds,*
    Charles Mackay, 1852

challenge, usually based on an insult, directly to the gentleman who had offended him.

To decline a challenge was often equated to defeat by forfeiture, and was sometimes even regarded as dishonourable. Prominent and famous individuals ran an especial risk of being challenged to duels. The challenged gentleman chose the weapons for the duel and the place, or 'field of honour.' The location had to be a place where they could duel without being arrested. Each side would bring a doctor and seconds. The seconds would try to settle the dispute between the combatants with an apology, if this succeeded the dispute was considered honourably settled and everyone went home.

There were three positions for a pistol duel. In the first the parties stood back-to-back with loaded weapons in hand and walked a set number of paces, before turning to face their opponent, and shooting. The more serious the insult, the fewer the paces. In the second, a set distance was paced, usually thirty paces. At a given signal the combatant awarded first fire advanced ten yards and then fired. In the third a set number of paces were measured, around ten or twelve was usual, the combatants would face one another and 'present' and at a given signal they would 'fire.' If they missed they reloaded and tried again. A misfire was not counted as a shot.

A custom had grown of either one of the duellists discharging their pistol into the air if they wished to end the duel without harming the other contestant or appearing cowardly. The Irish Code Duello forbade this, and some years later people complained that the Irish Code was far too deadly, just for the necessary business of satisfying honour among the Gentry.

Some authorities turned a blind eye to duelling unless someone was killed. The authorities in London certainly clamped down on duels and many a duellist found himself up before the judge having been apprehended on his way to a duel (the constable acting on information received). Mostly these gentlemen were bound over to keep the peace. *The Times* newspaper reported in 1819[5] on *"A Duel prevented in Low Life,"* when two gentleman's servants on their way to a duel with two borrowed, loaded, horse pistols, were apprehended by a Marylebone constable who 'had received information' of what was to take place. They were bound over in the sum of £50, all over a five shilling bet! This was seen as an affront, that

---

5    *The Times*, Friday, February 5, 1819; pg 3

servants should dare encroach on the 'Gentry' domain! Nearly every duel reported seemed to be different.

In Jamaica in 1784 a duel[6] between a planter and a surveyor took place. The argument had started about the choice of a Negro slave, words came to blows and the blows produced the 'challenge.' At their meeting each had fired one shot and missed, at which stage the seconds interposed, but to no avail, and having failed left the field. The two contestants fired their pistols a second time and the planter received a slight flesh wound. They reloaded their pistols for a third time and this time the surveyor was mortally wounded. The coroner's inquest returned a verdict of, 'Wilful murder by persons unknown.'

London in 1786 saw a duel[7] between an Army Chaplain and a Naval Officer in a field, near Paddington, which had better consequences, despite the discharge of two pistols each. The Naval gentleman suffered a slight flesh wound, the seconds stepped in, and the affair was amicably settled there and then.

Also in 1786, in Ireland, two gentlemen agreed to meet in a room and fight a duel[8]. They tossed up to see who fired first. Mr Freeman won the toss and fired first but missed his opponent Mr Hull, who then fired and hit Mr Freeman in the breast. Unfortunately he died eight hours later.

From a confined room in Ireland to the free air over Paris. In 1808 a duel[9] took place from hot air balloons with the combatants intent on puncturing each others balloon with blunderbusses. This, one combatant managed to do, and sent his adversary and second plummeting to their death.

Paris again, two bankers Manuel and Beaumont were living near Paris in 1821[10]. Manuel, a married Polish Jew, was very wealthy. Beaumont, a native of Genoa, was unmarried, and possessed a large fortune. He had seduced Manuel's wife. Manuel found proof of his wife's infidelity and, after a violent argument with Beaumont in Paris, issued a 'challenge.' It was agreed, in the terms of the meeting, that one at least, should not survive the combat. Manuel offered forgiveness to his frail wife, if she

6    *The Times*, Tuesday January 18, 1785; pg 3
7    *The Times*, Wednesday, March 22, 1786; pg 2
8    *The Times*, Tuesday, April 25, 1786; pg 3
9    *The Times*, Monday, July 18, 1808; pg 4
10   *The Times*, Monday, April 16, 1821; pg 3

would abandon Beaumont. She declined. Manuel was killed at first shot. He was deeply mourned by all classes. The remains of Manuel were refused burial by the clergy, because of the manner of his death. The church was one of the few early opponents of the duel.

Having said earlier that the combatants preferred a secluded place to duel, this duel in Southern Ireland in 1808 seems to have drawn the crowds. It was between two good friends, a Mr Colclough and a Mr Alcock. They were rival candidates for a seat in Parliament. Mr Alcock had obtained the favour of a lady, who owned an estate, with *'Forty shillings a year'* tenants, who had a vote. The tenants preferred Mr Colclough to Mr Alcock and voted for Mr Colclough. This was resented by Alcock's side. Mr Colclough did not refuse their votes. Before the opening of the poll the following day, the two gentlemen met. Hundreds were present, including twelve County Magistrates. Colclough was shot through the heart at first fire, and fell dead. In a few hours, Alcock was returned duly elected. He was tried at Wexford, for murder,[11] and acquitted. The results of the duel and trial took their toll on Alcock. He became depressed and died, a mental and physical wreck, in a Madhouse.

In Edinburgh in 1815[12] two Gentlemen were apprehended by the Sheriff's officers having fought a bloodless duel. The participants and the seconds were ordered to find security to keep the peace and the Sheriff then fined them twenty five guineas each which he said should be given to the local Lunatic Asylum, 'as from its nature, an institution best entitled to a fine derived from such a source.'

Even in the days of sword fights monarchs like James I and Charles I were trying to prevent duels. The Court of Chivalry heard many cases relating to 'scandalous words provocative of a duel.'

Perhaps[13] King Frederick the Great of Prussia had the best idea. He hated duelling but permitted it in the army provided the duellists would fight in the presence of the whole battalion of infantry drawn up to see fair play. The battalion was instructed that if one of the combatants fell then they were to shoot the other immediately. It was said that the King's stance put an end to duelling in his army.

11    *The Times*, Tuesday, April 5, 1808; pg 4
12    *The Times*, Wednesday, February 22, 1875; pg 3
13    *Memoirs of Extraordinary Popular Delusions and the Madness of Crowds*, Charles Mackay, 1852

The Emperor[14] Joseph II of Austria was as firm as Frederick and the following explains his views on the subject: 'I will suffer no duelling in my army. I despise the principles of those who attempt to justify the practice.' During the Peninsular War, Wellington actually forbade his officers to kill each other off in duels – he thought the French were already doing a good job of that.

In 1712, Augustus[15] King of Poland, issued an edict which decreed the punishment of death against principals and seconds, and minor punishments against the bearers of a challenge. An edict was also published at Munich, in 1773, according to which both principals and seconds, even in duels where no one was either killed or wounded, should be hanged, and their bodies buried at the foot of the gallows.

The King of Naples issued an ordinance against duelling in 1838, in which, 'the punishment of death is decreed against all concerned in a fatal duel. The bodies of those killed, and of those who may be executed in consequence, are to be buried in unconsecrated ground, and without any religious ceremony'.

The authorities were being pushed by public opinion to prevent duels and Benjamin Franklin and Queen Victoria added their voices, together with the Vatican. Eventually duelling with pistols fell out of favour. Another factor was that people who received a 'challenge' and did not want to fight, reported the 'challenge' to the authorities as did people who heard there was a chance of a duel. The 'challengers' were usually bound over to keep the peace for a year.

An amusing tale of a duel was told in 1866[16] about two Gentlemen from Newcastle-under-Lyme. It started with a game of billiards and a dispute over a shot which led to the 'challenge.' It must be stated that only the challenger was in earnest about this and had even made his will. The others thought it a joke. Two pistols were borrowed, these were loaded by the seconds who only put in the powder and dispensed with the bullets. They adjourned to the back garden and placed thirty paces apart. At a given signal they both fired and the challenged fell. His second ran to him and

14   *Memoirs of Extraordinary Popular Delusions and the Madness of Crowds,*
     Charles Mackay, 1852
15   *Memoirs of Extraordinary Popular Delusions and the Madness of Crowds,*
     Charles Mackay, 1852
16   *The Times,* Saturday, June 23, 1866; pg 12

very carefully smeared his face with red colouring which looked like blood. The other stood still, ashen faced. The 'body' was carried indoors and a surgeon sent for. There was no surgeon available! The challenger bemoaned the fact that he had killed this man and cried aloud. The 'corpse' could stand it no longer. He laughed and jumped up frightening the challenger even more, who, eventually, realised he had been hoaxed and rushed out of the house to the laughter of his friends. Whether they stayed friends is not recorded. This shows that people were not taking duelling with guns seriously anymore.

Having said that, *The Times* newspaper in 1842 carried an advert for life assurance. It said, 'Policies of 12 months standing are not affected by suicide, duelling, &c.; and assigned policies are valid from the date thereof, should death ensue from any of these causes. This is an advantage not offered by any other assurance company, in the event of death by suicide, duelling &c. the whole amount assured will be paid. This fact is of too great importance to be overlooked.'

# Chapter 3

## Duels in Wales

Many duels were recorded in Wales thanks to the newspapers of the time. A duel[17] took place in Pembrokeshire in 1799 between John James of Pantseison and Samuel Simmons Fortune. S. S. Fortune died of his wounds and following a coroner's verdict of 'Wilful Murder,' James fled to the continent. He did return many years later to inherit his estate and subsequently became a respectable colonel in the Pembrokeshire Militia.

In 1800 a duel[18] between a Major Armstrong of the 11th Regiment of Foot, and his challenger Captain Wilson of the Royal Artillery, took place on a Sunday morning, in the wood of Llandaff Castle, near Cowbridge in South Wales. The ground was measured at nine paces distance from each other. They each fired two pistols and missed both times. The duel then ended amicably and they both went home.

North Wales did have its duels and one took place between[19] a Mr Hilton and Mr Wolstenholme in Flintshire in December 1807, and also one between[20] a Mr Green and a Mr Dogherty who met at Holyhead in March 1818. There are no records of the consequences of either duel.

The newspapers of the day were very fond of reporting duels and only using initials, or giving surnames with missing letters. To the locals it must have been obvious who the combatants were.

In January 1817 Mr T.[21] of Swansea met Mr H. of Briton Ferry at Crumlin Burrows and in June of the same year Capt. P.[22] RN fought a Mr W. at Brecon and the following month Col[23]. S-r-k-e met J. B. W-n-t at Laugharne.

---

17  *Princelings, Privilege & Power*, L. Baker-Jones, Gomer, pg 205.
18  *The Times*, Thursday, August 14, 1800, pg 3
19  *Cambrian Index*, 26 December 1807
20  *Cambrian Index*, 21 March 1818
21  *Cambrian Index*, 25 January 1817
22  *Cambrian Index*, 14 June 1817
23  *Cambrian Index*, 5 July 1817

One Sunday night in January 1822 the town of Neath was buzzing with excitement and some alarm because of the duel[24] that was to take place the following morning between two attorney's clerks. Despite all attempts at reconciliation they met on the 'field of honour.' Much to the amusement of everyone concerned neither party had provided pistols! The contestants expressed disappointment, but their seconds managed to persuade them to return home, without the satisfaction of killing or being killed.

Cilycwm, Llandovery, was the site of a duel[25] in November 1822 between Captain Rice of Llwynybrain and Mr Charles Bishop of Kington. Mr Bishop fired first and missed. Captain Rice discharged his pistol into the air and the affair ended there and then. Just down the road at Llandilo on Tuesday the 8th June 1824, S. F. Gwynne Esq. of Glanbrân Park and L. Lewis[26] Esq. met and exchanged a case of pistols each, fortunately without effect. The pair had met over the conduct of Mr Gwynne's manservant.

An undated duel[27] took place on Tavernspite mountain on the Pembrokeshire/Carmarthenshire border when two un-named contestants met at a distance of twenty paces. A local gentleman, Captain Childs, was the second to one combatant and substituted peas for shot in the pistols so that neither gentleman would be hurt! They obviously saw the funny side of it and shared their cherry brandy before happily going home in the post chaise.

Tavernspite mountain seemed a popular place to duel. During the Pembrokeshire Elections in 1831 Sir John Owen of Orielton defeated R. Fulke Greville to become MP for Pembrokeshire. John Jones of Ystrad, M.P. for Carmarthen, a supporter of Sir John, met R. F. Greville in Haverfordwest and insulted Greville. Greville then challenged Jones to a duel and they met at Tavernspite on 22nd October 1831. Greville's shot missed Jones[28], who fired his pistol in the air, and refused to apologise.

Two young men from Aberystwyth had an argument one Saturday evening in December 1834. As nothing would settle the affair but a duel[29], a challenge was given and accepted; seconds were chosen as was the ground, Builth Mawr, just outside the town. On Monday morning the

24    *Cambrian Index*, 5 January 1822
25    *Cambrian Index*, 11 November 1822
26    *Cambrian Index*, 26 June 1824
27    *Memories of Half a Century* by Owen Square, undated, chapt. 47, pg 116 & 117, Local Characters
28    *Carmarthenshire Antiquarian Society Transactions, Vol XXII*, pg 13
29    *Cambrian Index*, 13 December 1834

parties and their seconds met there and as soon as it was light the distance of twelve yards was measured and the combatants took their stations and at a given signal fired – happily without effect. Not happy with the result, they reloaded their pistols and fired again – without effect. The two heroes decided that enough was enough, and that they had proved they were gentlemen, shook hands, and that was the end of the dispute.

The Cambrian reported on the 6th of April 1839 that a sensation had been caused in Tenby when a duel took place at Cumfreston Farm early the previous Monday. The antagonists were the Mayor of the Borough of Tenby, William Richards Esq., and William Mannix Esq., also of Tenby. They met on a matter relative to parochial affairs. Mannix fired first and shot Richards in the side who then fired in the air. Mr Richards was taken to the farmhouse and then home by post chaise accompanied by Mr Smyth his second.

The paper then reported, 'He now lies in a precarious state, the ball not having been extracted.' He was attended by three or four of the best medical men of the area. Mr Mannix and his second, Mr Beecher, made their escape from the ground.

The same paper reported the following week,[30] 'The gloomy forebodings of last week by the result of the late duel have disappeared and the town has resumed its wonted cheerfulness as Mr Richards is recovering from the effects of his wound. Too much praise cannot be bestowed on his medical attendants for their skilful treatment and unwearied attention.'

Many duels never took place despite 'challenges' being sent. Usually the strong arm of the law caught up with the challenger and he was indicted for trying to incite a duel. Sometimes the sentence was, bound over to keep the peace, and sometimes a twelve month gaol sentence.

A letter[31] sent to Mr G. P. Watkins of Tenby in June 1810 and printed in the Gazette in August was not couched in very friendly terms. It said, 'George Watkins, this is to give you notice when you come to Laugharne in March to bring pistols with you ... my pistol is ready. If I kill you, no jury will condemn me, it is time to send such a villain out of the world ... your father was a very great villain, but you are 10,000 times worse. ... It is a great pity you suffer to live so long to torment honest people – that Griffith the

30   Cambrian Index, 13 April 1839
31   Cambrian Index, 11 August 1810

supervisor has made you ten times bigger villain … I hope you will come soon … and the 'divil' will soon have you then, it is no use to let you live much longer for you are going worse and worse every day.' It was signed by Humfrey Peney of Langhorn Marsh, but the paper carried a reward of fifty pounds 'and her Majesty's pardon' for the discovery of the writer's name.

In April 1811 at Carmarthen Assizes[32] an indictment was preferred against John Horsley of Llan, Llandeveylog, on the prosecution of E. Davids of Carmarthen for using language calculated to provoke him to fight a duel. The court did not deem the language and circumstances sufficient to support the indictment and directed the jury to acquit the defendant.

Two Gentlemen[33] of Abergavenny were not so fortunate. In 1818 Capt. Ellis and Mr Price were prosecuted for 'sending and taking a challenge' to General William Kinsey to fight a duel. It arose over a trespass issue, when General Kinsey was coursing over Capt. Ellis' land. The challenge was refused but the court decided that there had been some provocation and that Gen. Kinsey had said he was not afraid to meet any man. Ellis and Price had been in custody for many months before proceedings ended. The court ruled that, 'The rule of criminal information should be made absolute and, that Capt. Ellis should keep the peace for two years with a surety for two thousand pounds.'

When they were released[34] they were given the greatest welcome that has been seen in the area for many years by the people of Abergavenny. The mail coach was met a mile from the town by a large crowd of people. The horses were taken out of the coach and it was pulled by manpower to the Angel Inn and the celebrations went on all night.

Again in Monmouthshire, at the County Assizes in September 1824 a Bill of Indictment[35] was preferred by Thomas Jones Phillips and found a 'true bill' by the Grand Jury against Henry Smith of Newport, Attorney at Law, and Richard Reece, of the same place, Attorney at Law, for a conspiracy to libel Mr Phillips and to instigate him to fight a duel.

Having looked at a variety of duels, including those that happened in Wales, and their consequences we arrive at the 'Last Fatal Duel in Wales.'

32   *Cambrian Index*, 20 April 1811
33   *Cambrian Index*, 6 June 1818
34   *Cambrian Index*, 20 February 1819
35   *Cambrian Index*, 11 September 1824

# Chapter 4

## The Last Fatal Duel in Wales

## 'Alas! Poor Heslop'

This is the final line of the epitaph on Thomas Heslop's grave in Llandyfriog Churchyard, near Adpar, Newcastle Emlyn. He, a 'West Indian Gentleman,' was the tragic victim of the 'Last Fatal Duel' that duel took place on the 10th September 1814. He was buried on the 12th September.

The story of this 'Duel' has been told many times over the years and 'colour' added at various 'tellings.'

I first remember being told the story around 1944 in a class lesson by Mr D. W. Thomas, the head teacher of our local primary school. I also remember being an 'extra' in 'The Last Duel' being acted out at a pageant on the Castle grounds in 1951 together with the 'First Printing Press' and the 'Rebecca Riots.'

Similar versions of this tale have been told ever since. The duel has been featured more than once on TV yet only 'bits' of the true story have ever been used – no one has told the full tale – and I am as guilty as anyone in this matter.

The purpose of this book is to try to put the record straight, as far as is possible. I will relate the 'old' version first and then tell it as it happened from the available contemporary evidence. What was the truth? We will never know. Even the 'new' version leaves many questions unanswered. Some of these will be addressed later. Some will still remain unanswered.

# Chapter 5

## The 'Old' Version of the Duel

This version of the story tells how Thomas Heslop, a black gentleman from the West Indies, living in Carmarthen came to Newcastle Emlyn in September 1814. He stayed at the local hostelry in Adpar, the Old Salutation Inn, where it was said he had taken a fancy to the buxom barmaid.

A few days later he, with others, was invited by John Beynon a local solicitor, of Llwyncadfor Farm, to a partridge shoot at Danwarren Dingle between Adpar and Llandyfriog.

Following that day's sport the shooting party were further invited by John Beynon to dine at the Old Salutation Inn that night.

After dinner the conversation turned to that day's shoot. Thomas Heslop said he wasn't very pleased with his day's sport as the 'Cardiganshire men present' had not let him shoot when and where he wanted.

John Beynon tried to play this down by offering Heslop more wine but Heslop insisted on raising the matter yet again and got very angry.

John Beynon tried to defuse the situation by passing derogatory remarks about the buxom barmaid. This further incensed Thomas Heslop, he then called John Beynon some names and challenged him to a duel.

It was probably the last duel in Wales and took place at Danwarren Fields between Adpar and Llandyfriog in Cardiganshire early on Saturday morning the 10th September 1814. John Walters was Thomas Heslop's second and James Hughes was John Beynon's.

The duelists stood back to back over a small stream and were meant to walk ten paces, turn, and, at a signal, shoot. In the event John Beynon turned at five paces and shot Thomas Heslop in the back, killing him. Death was certified by Surgeon John Williams of Newcastle Emlyn, who was present at the duel.

Thomas Heslop was buried in the Churchyard to the west of the tower at Llandyfriog.

Some time later John Beynon, James Hughes and John Walters were all charged with the manslaughter of Thomas Heslop at Cardigan Court. Hughes and Walters were acquitted and John Beynon fined. It is said that as a solicitor he knew all the local JP's and gentry and this was the reason for his light sentence. In fact several of the local landowners spoke up for him at the trial.

The story then continues to say that when John Beynon was set free the people of Newcastle Emlyn were so incensed with the verdict that Beynon had to go into hiding in a cellar in Bridge Street, Newcastle Emlyn before eventually fleeing to America.

Various articles and newspaper columns have addressed the duel over the years[36]. It was suggested most forcibly by one lady that the duel had been fought because Beynon and Heslop were in love with the same barmaid. The same correspondent says that Heslop was in Newcastle Emlyn for the fishing! One of the writers, John y Gwas, from Drefach, a village just outside Newcastle Emlyn, is the only one to mention the Judge's Notes. It seems that no one has ever read them through, until now.

36   *NLW*, Daniel Parry-Jones, notes and newspaper cuttings, 66 xiii

# Chapter 6

## The New Version of the Duel

Now let us go back to the beginning of the story and using the Judge's private notes from the trial[37], the Inquest report[38], the Indictment[39], Criminal Registers[40] and letters written at the time try to put some semblance of truth into the tale.

Thomas Heslop was of West Indian origin [Burial Register in Llandyfriog Church] and according to a letter[41] written at the time by Lettice Rogers, sister-in-law to Surgeon John Williams, Heslop had a brother living in Jamaica. Thomas Heslop had lived at Carmarthen for some four or five months and was a well educated man, judging from a letter[42] written to the *Carmarthen Journal* in June 1814.

He arrived in Newcastle Emlyn some five weeks prior to the duel for the purpose of 'enjoying the country sport of shooting.' He was staying somewhere in the town, probably at the Salutation (whether it was the Old Salutation in Adpar or the Salutation Hotel in Bridge Street, across the river at Newcastle Emlyn is not known).

Thomas Heslop had been invited by some of the local gentry to participate in a partridge shoot at Danwarren Dingle near Llandyfriog on Thursday the 8th September 1814.

In the evening after the shoot, John Beynon, a local solicitor, invited the party to dine at his house. Rees Thomas was one of the guests and from his evidence at the trial we are told what happened at John Beynon's house.

---

37  See Appendix 4, *NLW.* Volume XX1 (212D) for the Autumn Sessions 1814, and Spring 1815, Cardigan (pp 46–55) also *The Volume XX1 (212D)* regarding the trial was transcribed by George Eyre Evans and published in the *Carmarthenshire Antiquarian Society Transactions Volume XV11* Parts XL111, XL1V 1923-1924, pg 33–36.

38  See Appendix 1, NLW. *Crime and Punishment* File No 4/912/3 Document No 47

39  See Appendix 2, NLW. *Crime and Punishment* File No 4/912/3 Document No 5

40  NLW, Film 854, *Criminal Registers 1805–92*, pg 23 Cardigan Spring Sessions 1815.

41  See Appendix 6. *Carmarthen Antiquarian Transactions*, Vol 12, pg 33

42  See Appendix 6. *Carmarthen Journal*, June 10, 1814 pg 1

Thomas Heslop was having a conversation about shooting with Mr Lewis of Dyffryn. Heslop was recounting his experiences when shooting with Mr Williams, Alderbrook Hall [Gwernant, Rhydlewis] a few days earlier. He had seen a great number of birds – partridge – but had very bad sport, he had only killed a brace or two that season [season started 1st September] but had shot close to the house of Mr Williams. Mr Lewis replied that it was not acceptable to shoot on any gentleman's land if you were not acquainted with him and had not been introduced.

Thomas Heslop's reply to this was that he would shoot wherever he liked but Mr Lewis convinced him he shouldn't. Mr Lewis was sitting on the right of John Beynon and Thomas Heslop on his left. John Beynon did his best to turn the conversation away from shooting. George Phillips and James Hughes had joined the group and together with Rees Thomas stayed to supper.

About 1.00am Thomas Heslop entered on the subject of shooting again without John Beynon introducing it. He said he'd had very bad sport that day and thought that he should sport when and where he pleased. He did not care for the Cardigan(shire) gentlemen.

Heslop objected to Owen (Beynon's man) killing more game than any other man in the country and preventing him (Heslop) killing game. This together with his bad experience at Alderbrook Hall was the reason Heslop was upset.

John Beynon then took him by the hand and asked him to drop the subject as it was a disagreeable one to him and he was sure that he (Heslop) would feel differently in the morning. Heslop seemed to have got a bee in his bonnet and kept on that he would sport where and when he pleased and that he disliked the Cardigan gentlemen.

John Beynon kept his cool and told Thomas Heslop that he would spoil his own sport and lose the pleasure he had come for. At that Thomas Heslop got very violent and John Beynon offered him some more wine hoping to diffuse matters. This Thomas Heslop declined.

John Beynon then wished Thomas Heslop 'Good night' but he did not take the hint. Instead he turned to Rees Thomas and asked him if he would be his friend. Rees Thomas declined. Heslop then appealed to James Hughes, who also declined. [Friend in this sense could mean 'second' for duelling].

Thomas Heslop then turned on John Beynon and said with his fist clenched, as a man in a passion, 'You are a damned villain and scoundrel and you shall answer for this.' Heslop repeated this two or three times.

John Beynon rang the bell and ordered his servant to conduct Thomas Heslop out of the house. The servant laid hold of Heslop's arm and led him out. Rees Thomas slept at Beynon's house that night. John Beynon told Rees Thomas in the morning that he felt no anger, only regret.

John Beynon in evidence said he had received a 'challenge' next morning, Friday the 9th September, from Thomas Heslop. He had replied that he was engaged that day but would meet him on the next. He did this to give an opportunity for tempers to cool and desired James Hughes to make it so. He said that Heslop's continuing argument about where and when he could shoot and calling him a 'damned villain and scoundrel' was a great and unprovoked insult. He (Beynon) had tried to make amicable terms with Heslop but he wouldn't have it.

This was utter provocation on the part of Heslop, especially the 'challenge' which arrived next morning. Nothing but Beynon's life would satisfy Heslop and the only alternative to the 'challenge' would leave him (Beynon) begging on his knees and branded a coward.

Edward Pridham, a Chemyst and Druggist of Newcastle Emlyn giving evidence said that on the day following the argument he had a conversation with Thomas Heslop, whom he knew and had sported with previously. Thomas Heslop told him that he'd had a quarrel with John Beynon and had sent him a 'challenge.'

Pridham tried to get Heslop to settle and stay cool. Heslop's answer to that was that he would not accept an apology unless John Beynon was on his knees and then he would post him on every door as a coward. Pridham again advised Heslop to stay cool and as he got up to leave he requested Heslop to fire low.

Heslop's answer was, 'I shall shoot him through the heart, if it is in my power, and then I shall call that rascall Hughes out.'

Saturday the 10th of September was the fateful day on which they met at Danwarren Dingle; John Walters acted as Thomas Heslop's second and James Hughes as Beynon's.

In court Beynon's account of the duel went like this, 'We agreed we should fire the distance of twelve paces [they stood facing one another twelve paces apart] and that James Hughes should give the word of command.'

Heslop then complained the light was rather too bright for his eyes and I said, 'I will give you the choice of ground,' and we exchanged positions.

When the word, 'Present' was given we both 'Presented' and before the word 'Fire,' Heslop said 'Stop.'

James Hughes then takes up the story: 'John Beynon recovered his pistol obviously expecting some explanation, instead of which Thomas Heslop brought his pistol down to level at Beynon's body and said, 'Go on,' on which the word 'Fire' was given. The pan on Heslop's pistol did not recede but the cock went down. If it had fired, the bullet would have struck John Beynon in the heart as the pistol was pointing directly at it. At the same time on the command 'Fire,' John Beynon fired his pistol and fatally shot Thomas Heslop.'

John Walters in evidence said the bullet was the cause of Heslop's death. Surgeon John Williams giving evidence said that on Saturday, the morning of the duel, while he was dressing and getting ready to come downstairs, James Hughes arrived and inquired if he was at home. When John Williams reached the door, Hughes requested that he go to a certain place in the dingle called Cwm Danwarren. Could he please make haste as Thomas Heslop was shot and take his instruments and every other means in his power, to render him every assistance.

Surgeon John Williams left his house and James Hughes stayed there. On Newcastle Emlyn bridge he met John Walters who also desired him to make all the haste he could and he would show Williams the place where Thomas Heslop lay.

John Walters went with him part of the way and they met John Beynon. John Walters spoke to John Beynon, suggesting that he take himself off as soon as he could, but Beynon made no reply. Walters walked with John Williams as far as the Turnpike Road which led to the spot. This was the Cardigan to Lampeter Turnpike and it ran from Cwmcou to the top of Adpar Hill before descending and turning left along the road below Emlyn Cottage before descending again towards Llandyfriog about half a mile from Adpar. There was no road, only a rough lane from Newcastle Emlyn bridge to the Turnpike, Danwarren Dingle and Llandyfriog.

At the Turnpike John Williams told John Walters to return to Newcastle Emlyn. Walters left and John Williams walked to the spot where Thomas Heslop lay. Williams went on to say that when he found Heslop he was dead and cold, lying on his back. He examined the cause of Heslop's death and found a pistol bullet had penetrated his right side, gone through his left side and was loose in his flannel waistcoat.

A number of people had gathered by now and the corpse was carried to the 'Salutation Inn' at Adpar.

From information on other duels it was common practice to take the body to the nearest hostelry where the inquest was then held.

On his return to Newcastle Emlyn, John Williams met John Walters in virtually the same place as when they parted. Walters, in his conversation with John Williams, said it had been an unfortunate event. He had tried to put a stop to it but poor Heslop was determined on it. He had pointed out to Heslop the impropriety of the ridiculous demand suggested (having Beynon pleading on his knees) and had suggested that Heslop should fire low.

Heslop had replied that he would fire high and would be damned if he would not fire through Beynon's heart if he could, and afterwards he would 'have the other scoundrel out,' but had not mentioned any names.

John Williams went on to say that he had visited John Beynon at home and given him the result of the verdict of the jury who 'had sat on the body.'

The verdict of the inquisition carried out by Cardiganshire Coroner William Williams of Blaendyffryn was, 'That a person unknown, did, feloniously, wilfully, and of his malice aforethought, kill and murder Thomas Heslop.'

On the following day, Sunday, he again visited Beynon who said that it had been an unfortunate accident, he could not avoid it in duty to his character and honour. When he had received the written 'challenge' he felt compelled to it.

# Chapter 7

## The Court of Great Sessions

At the 1815 Cardigan Spring Great Sessions, on the 22nd March, the trial of John Beynon, John Walters and James Hughes took place in front of the Chief Justice of Wales, Serjeant Samuel Heywood, who had been appointed to the Carmarthen circuit, which included Cardigan and Haverfordwest, in 1807.

All three were charged with murder in the original indictment. This was changed to manslaughter, probably by William Owen, who was the Attorney General for the Carmarthen circuit and had been in post since March[43] 1814. He was responsible for reading and approving all indictments. Every change on the indictment was crossed through and initialled by William Owen.

The charge was as follows:

'On September 10th 1814, John Beynon for shooting Thomas Heslop with a leaden bullet discharged from a pistol; John Walters and James Hughes present for abetting and assisting John Beynon in so shooting.'

Appearing for the prosecution was the Attorney General and Bligh, and J. Jones and (not readable) for the prisoners.

Prosecutor was John Heslop. (*Whether this was the brother referred to in Lettice Rogers' letter or another relative is not known.*)

The Attorney General said the charge had been reduced from murder to manslaughter and there was no 'malice in principal.'

Witnesses for the prosecution were Surgeon John Williams and his son-in-law, Edward Pridham, Chemyst & Druggist, both of Bridge Street, Newcastle Emlyn.

The evidence given by the witnesses has been used to build up the story, as and when it happened, and this evidence will not be repeated here.

43   *Cambrian Index* March 19, 1814

The 'challenge' was produced in court and the handwriting of Thomas Heslop was proved. The 'challenge' was then read. *(Unfortunately there is no record of what it said.)*

John Beynon was an attorney at law in Newcastle Emlyn and a landowner in Adpar and the Teifi Valley and his many friends among the local landowners and gentry gave evidence of his good character in court.

*Sir John Owen:* Has known Mr Beynon a great number of years, very intimately: particularly good, mild and humane disposition.'

*Mr Powell of Nanteos:* 'Six or seven years; perfectly mild, humane and excellent character – cannot say this enough.'

*Mr Lewes of Llysnewydd:* 'Had known Beynon twenty years, remarkably mild and humane and gentlemanly in his manners.'

*Capt. Colby:* 'Had known Beynon a good many years; remarkably mild and humane gentleman. Sober and cautious and circumspect in every respect.'

*Colonel Brigstocke:* 'Great number of years, particularly mild and good tempered. Never observed disposition to quarrel.'

*Thomas Lloyd of Bronwydd:* 'Several years, a great number. As gentlemanly a man in manners as I ever knew. A humane gentle man.'

*Mr Lloyd Williams of Alderbrook Hall:* 'Fourteen years, very gentlemanly, mild and gentle, not the least disposition to quarrel.'

*Mr Lewis of Dyffryn:* 'From a child. Particularly refined, particularly mild and gentle. He got drunk with him very often, never quarrelsome even when drunk.'

*Captain Brigstocke:* 'Fourteen or fifteen years. Good tempered, quiet, inoffensive.'

*Mr Price:* 'Many years. Remarkably mild humane gentleman.'

# Chapter 8

## *The Verdict of the Court*

The outcome of the trial was that John Walters and James Hughes were found not guilty of manslaughter.

John Beynon was found guilty of manslaughter but only fined 1/- [one shilling], 5p[44]. He was imprisoned until the fine was paid.

It is assumed that the fine was paid into court and John Beynon walked free after the proceedings.

44   *NLW, Film 854, Criminal Registers 1805–92*  pg 23 Cardigan Spring Sessions
     1815

# Chapter 9

## Thomas Heslop's Grave

Thomas Heslop's grave in Llandyfriog Churchyard is thirty yards to the west of the bell tower. He was buried by the Vicar Rev. John Williams on Monday the 12th of September 1814 only two days after the shooting. The stone is more than a little weathered by now and the inscription is getting harder to read.

The inscription reads:

**SACRED**
**To the memory of**
**THOMAS HESLOP**
**Born 27th June 1780**
**Died 10th Sept 1814.**
**Alas! Poor Heslop**

Yes, *'Alas! Poor Heslop,'* – the last man to die in a duel in Wales.

The dates on his grave give Thomas Heslop as aged 34 and the burial register records it as 36. Who paid for Heslop's burial? As the age is different on the gravestone and a date of birth appended, it is possible that perhaps the Heslop family themselves paid for the gravestone. When was the built-up box grave erected, and by whom? Was it one of the landed gentry with something on his conscience? It is one of only two graves of its type in the churchyard. There are one or two similar graves in other local churchyards.

One would not have expected to find Thomas Heslop buried in this type of grave. For a visitor to this Country who had no relatives here, a simple stone or cross would have been more usual. This type of 'box' grave is common among the gentry though more often than not sheets of slate are used and not blocks of stone as here. Who was the mysterious person who occasionally put flowers on the grave?

# Chapter 10

# Conclusion

I have now recorded the full story of the Beynon / Heslop duel from all the known documentation. The archived documents from the court case, the inquest, the indictment, the Judge's notes, the gaol files and any contemporary correspondence have been perused and are added in the appendices.

The duel was not reported in the newspapers of that time. Perhaps it was suppressed; with so many of the 'gentry' appearing as witnesses and John Beynon being 'gentry' and also part of the local legal system.

It is strange to find that the trial that followed Beynon's, when the defendant, Evan Davies[45], was sentenced to death for burglary, then later reprieved, was fully reported. It is also interesting to note that the premises he burgled were the 'Old Salutation Inn' in Adpar about a month after the duel took place.

The facts of the 'Old' story told about the John Beynon – Thomas Heslop duel had only a grain of truth. That the 'challenge' had arisen over a dispute about shooting rights was correct. The embellishments added to the story at various tellings were done to make it more interesting. There was no mention in the evidence of any earlier argument in the Salutation Inn over the buxom qualities of the barmaid. The evidence states that the argument took place in Beynon's house, Adpar Hill, and I cannot find any connection to link Beynon with Llwyncadfor, a farm north of Llandyfriog.

The burial register in Llandyfriog Church gives Heslop as West Indian, and Lettice Rogers' letter to her sister said he had a brother living in Jamaica. I cannot say whether Thomas Heslop was black or not. That speculation did give rise to an interesting anecdote, told all those years ago, that Thomas Heslop's ghost walked in Cwm Danwarren on dark, windy, nights, but because it was black you could not see it!

---

45   NLW. Volume XXI (212D) for the Autumn Sessions 1814, and Spring 1815, Cardigan (pp 46-55) and NLW, *Crime and Punishment* File No. 4/912/3 Document No. 57

George Eyres Evans, Historian and Antiquarian, tells the Duel story in his book[46] written around 1903 in a piece about Llandyfriog churchyard. Somehow he managed to get the month of the duel and burial wrong, recording December instead of September. As G. E. Evans was so accurate in his observations it makes me think that it was just a slip of the pen, as he goes on to say, 'today, all we read is the simple inscription on the gravestone, with the exclamation: 'Alas! Poor Heslop.' Several books then repeated this mistake.

A reference in this and other[47] books that the duel took place in Cwm Danwarren 'a glen, hard by the church,' is also wrong, as the 'Cwm' is at least a mile from the church. It is referred to in the inquest report as Blaennant Dingle. The Dingle ran from Blaennant in the north to Danwarren in the south. There is a little stream in the 'Cwm' but there is no mention in the court evidence that they 'stood back to back, over a stream,' as suggested in the 'Old' version, or that 'Beynon turned and shot Heslop in the back from 5 paces.' The court evidence says, 'that they faced one another at a measured twelve paces.' The medical evidence, given by Surgeon John Williams and confirmed by the Inquest, shows that Heslop was shot in the right side, the ball exiting on his left side and ending up in his shirt. This certainly does not mean 'shot in the back!"

The fatal injury sustained by Heslop was a common injury in pistol duels and usually resulted in death, but not always instantaneous. It was said that an instantaneous death from this kind of injury was better than a lingering one when death was caused by peritonitis which was common in these injuries. The following are examples of this sort of injury.

In 1818 in London, Mr Rodd,[48] a surgeon, who examined a Lieutenant Bayley, who had been shot in a duel by Mr O'Callaghan, found that the ball had penetrated on his right side and had traversed to the left side and was almost out of the skin. This he removed. Lt. Bayley died later.

Also in London, in 1784, during the duel[49] between Frederick Thomas Esq. and the Hon. Cosmo Gordon, Thomas was mortally shot in the right

46   *Cardiganshire and its Antiquities*, George Eyre Evans, 1903. 'Llandyfriog Church' (See Appendix 5)
47   *Walks and Wanderings in County Cardigan, Llandyfriog*,
      E. K. Horsfall-Turner, chapter XVIII, pg 207-208 (see Appendix 5)
48   *The Times*, Thursday, January 15, 1818, pg 3
49   *Old Bailey Proceedings Online* (wwww.oldbaileyonline.org 18 May 2007)
      17 September, 1784, trial of Cosmo Gordon (t17840917-1)

side of the belly. The wound was the length of one inch, and the ball had penetrated sideways to a depth of fourteen inches. Frederick Thomas died a day later.

During the last duel on English soil, at Englefield Green near Windsor, between two Frenchmen, Frederick Cournet was fatally shot by Emmanuel Barthélémy in the right side the bullet coming out on the left[50] and being found later on the bed where he died.

A letter[51] written in Autumn 1814 a few weeks after the duel by Lettice Rogers, sister-in-law to John Williams, sent to another sister, describes the dinner and the duel.

It says, 'That the two seconds and Mr Beynon immediately absconded but are lately returned to resign themselves at the Assizes.'

It adds that, 'Mr. Beynon's second was his own clerk and Mr Heslop's the son of Mr Abel Walters of Beddgeraint who is also an attorney and lives in Newcastle Emlyn with his sister.'

The letter then says, 'Mr. John Williams was present at the duel and on his way home over the bridge threw the pistols into the river.'

The end statement in the above letter bothers me as it contradicts the court evidence. According to his evidence, John Williams was not present, but was called in after the duel. If he had been present at the duel he would have faced the same charges as the others. If he did throw the pistols in the river then it was on the way back from attending to Heslop. There is no record of where the pistols came from. Had one of the pistols been tampered with, or was it just bad maintenance of the firearm? Had John Williams, who was no stranger to firearms, and a former Captain and Adjutant[52] of the 'Tivyside Volunteer Corps' based in Cardigan, noticed something amiss? Had he disposed of the 'evidence'? We will never know.

Another piece of contradictory evidence from the letter says that, 'they immediately absconded,' yet John Williams says in his court evidence that he had acquainted John Beynon with the result of the inquest, 'Murder by persons unknown,' that same Saturday. He also saw him on the Sunday.

---

50 The Times, Friday, October 22, 1852, pg 8
51 See Appendix 6
52 See Appendix 6

The Inquest was held at the Salutation Tavern by William Williams, Surgeon, of Blaendyffryn, Bangor Teifi, one of the Cardiganshire coroners. Some years later Beynon drew up William Williams' will and was a beneficiary, as was Surgeon John Williams.

When the duel took place John Beynon was Treasurer of the County Stock of the County of Cardigan and a month later he was appointed Clerk of the Peace of the County of Cardigan in the room of Herbert Lloyd, and his second James Hughes was made Treasurer in his place. John Beynon was also appointed Solicitor for the County of Cardigan, with the 'usual salary.'

Was there collusion amongst the gentry to get Beynon a light sentence? Judging from the 'kind' words used by his friends 'the gentry,' they must all have attended the same elocution school! To have called ten of the local gentry to give John Beynon a character reference seems a little bit over the top. Perhaps the townspeople had a point in the 'Old' version. Parallels though can be drawn in this case with the duel trial of the Hon. Cosmo Gordon,[53] who, as mentioned earlier, was charged with killing Frederick Thomas Esq., called four character witnesses, 'and could call many more.' Their comments went like this:

*Capt Heron*: 'He was the most harmless man alive.'

*Mr Seton*: 'I have known him intimately for fifteen years. He is the last man in the world likely to be troublesome, quarrelsome, or anything but, was pleasant and agreeable.'

*Mr Dingwell*: 'I have known him since he was a child. He always was a good natured quiet man.'

*Mr Rackett*: 'I have known him thirty years, a humane, good natured, gentlemanlike man, for the whole time I have known him.' Perhaps they also attended the same elocution school as our gentry!

It was claimed by some sources that Beynon had hidden in the cellar of a saddler's shop in Bridge Street but with his contacts he did not need to do this anyway. I think Surgeon John Williams' evidence dispenses with that theory.

Beynon hailed from Llangynin near Carmarthen and had lived for many years near Pentrecourt in the Parish of Llangeler, and also near

53  Old Bailey Proceedings Online (wwww.oldbaileyonline.org, 18 May 2007)
    17 September, 1784, trial of Cosmo Gordon (t17840917-1)

Gorrig, Llandyssil. The Gorrig address, Troedrhiwpenyd, was the one used by him when he was made Clerk of the Peace of the County of Cardigan at the Quarter Sessions in Lampeterpontsteffan on the 19th October 1814.

Now let's turn to Heslop; judging from a letter he wrote in the *Carmarthen Journal*, answering a missive from a lady, he was well educated and would have been equal in class to the people he shot with. Duelling being the 'sport of the gentry' I cannot see Beynon accepting a challenge from a person of a lower class.

I have drawn a blank regarding Thomas Heslop in Jamaica. The Research and Information Department of the National Library of Jamaica have found a John Heslop (could it be the same one as prosecuted?) a land marker and searcher from Kingston. They also found an Alexander Heslop a Barrister at Law. I have no idea if these Heslops have anything at all to do with Thomas Heslop. The Jamaica Record Office has not unearthed anything. As nearly everyone else in the affair was a lawyer perhaps he was too.

The only facts that agree from the 'Old' version of events are the ones regarding Heslop's argument about his rights to shoot, his burial and subsequent gravestone in Llandyfriog Churchyard. The anomaly in his age on the gravestone and the burial register can probably be explained. His age, 36 years, would have been recorded in the burial register from hearsay, and if the John Heslop who prosecuted was a brother, he would have known the correct age, 34 years, and the date of birth, which was recorded on the gravestone.

The indictment of John Beynon, James Hughes and John Walters which was reduced from murder to manslaughter was common in duel trials.

'If this duel[54] was upon some sudden quarrel between the parties, and in heat of blood, that will reduce the offence to manslaughter,' was the Judge's summing up in the duel trial of Bennet Allen in 1782 who was accused of shooting Lloyd Dulany. In the Beynon / Heslop trial the records are silent about the reason why the charge was reduced to manslaughter but a probable reason is, that to convict[55] for 'murder malice aforethought,' had to be proved, that is, the Crown would have to prove beyond reasonable

54  Old Bailey Proceedings Online (wwww.oldbaileyonline.org, 18 May 2007)
    5 June, 1782, trial of Bennet Allen (t17820605-1)
55  Glyn Parry, National Library of Wales

doubt that Beynon had planned to murder Heslop which would have been very difficult especially as Heslop had issued the challenge.

From reading indictments from other duel trials the indictment itself appears to be standard procedure even to the price of the pistol!

'1782 ... malice aforethought[56], did make an assault; and that he, the said Bennet Allen, a certain pistol, of the value of five shillings, then and there charged with gunpowder and one leaden bullet, which pistol he, the said Bennet Allen, in his right-hand then and there had and held...' The one shilling fine in the Beynon trial was also common in the duel trials I have looked at; Bennet Allen was convicted of the manslaughter of Lloyd Dulany in 1782. 'The sentence of the court, for that offence of which you have been convicted, is that you be fined One Shilling, and imprisoned for Six Months.'

Later in 1796 Richard England, convicted of the manslaughter of William Peter Lee Rowlls, was told, 'The sentence of the Court upon you, therefore, is, that you be fined One Shilling[57], and imprisoned for twelve months.' Beynon was fortunate in not being imprisoned, perhaps it would have upset the 'system' if the Clerk to the Peace had been gaoled! Especially with so many influential and eloquent 'Gentry' friends, some of whom were Justices.

So much of the truth of this story hinges on the evidence of Surgeon John Williams. There is no quibble with the medical evidence, borne out by the inquest findings. The question remains, was John Williams present at the duel as is claimed by Lettice Rogers' letter to her sister? If he was he would have been charged with the manslaughter offence just like the other three. Did he throw the pistols in the river? Had they been tampered with? Was most of the story centred around the dinner made up to make Beynon an angel? We know from later accounts that he certainly was not. Leslie Baker-Jones in his book *Princelings, Privilege and Power* describes Beynon as one of the squire-lawyers who indulged in sharp practices and were the terror of ordinary folk. He further describes him as a rapacious lawyer who cost fellow landowners dearly by taking legal action against recalcitrant tenants and poachers. Clerks to the Courts, like Beynon, were paid through

56 Old Bailey Proceedings Online (www.oldbaileyonline.org, 18 May 2007)
5 June, 1782, trial of Bennet Allen (t17820605-1)
57 Old Bailey Proceedings Online (www.oldbaileyonline.org, 18 May 2007)
17 February 1796, trial of Richard England (t17960217-27)

fines and costs, consequently this led to prolonged litigation and verdicts weighted against tenants. It was said that the clerks had a hundred and one pretexts for further charges and Herbert Lloyd and John Beynon were notorious for their [58]unscrupulous methods.

To most of the questions raised we will never know the answers, but the one claim that has made this duel so interesting over the years, that he was shot in the back, we can answer, he certainly was not. Heslop was like a dog with a bone and he bit off more than he could chew by challenging Beynon.

Beynon was made out to be an angel from the testimony given by his Gentry witnesses. Later reports[59] suggest he was not and it is possible that the pistol was tampered with or had a very convenient misfire.

---

58    *Princelings, Privilege & Power*, L. Baker-Jones, Gomer, pg 270
59    *Princelings, Privilege & Power*, L. Baker-Jones, Gomer, pg 23

# Chapter 11

## The Bullet Handed Down

**By Richard Joseph John Crowe,**
**Gt-gt-gt-gt-Grandson of Surgeon John Williams.**

The bullet which Surgeon John Williams recovered from the body of the victim of the Beynon/Heslop duel in 1814, under such tragic and controversial circumstances, has been handed down through several generations of my family over almost two hundred years. It is indeed a 'gruesome relic'[60] as George Eyre Evans has stated, and has always induced a sense of horror, combined with questions concerning the duel and why it came to be kept. It remains for me to tell you something about the Williams and Pridham families and those who passed this bullet down from generation to generation. The bullet spent most of the Nineteenth Century in South Wales; part of the Twentieth Century in Dorset and part in Kent; and is now beginning its third century in a peaceful Oxfordshire town, wrapped in its familiar parchment and deposited in a box. It may have hoped to have shaken off its infamous past and entered a respectable retirement; but I fear that it is destined to become the centre of debate and enquiry once again, as a new generation examines the reasons why it came to be fired on that fateful morning.

---

60   Appendix 6. See extract from G. E. Evans, *Cardiganshire and its Antiquities*, 1903

# The Williams Family of Newcastle Emlyn

Surgeon John Williams and Anna Eliza Jones were married on 11th November 1782 at Cenarth[61]. Anna Eliza was born in 1763, a daughter of Owen and Ann Jones. Owen Jones was a Customs and Excise Officer in Newcastle Emlyn. John Williams, like his wife, almost certainly came from the minor gentry of Carmarthenshire, but his exact birthplace is not known. We know that he was apprenticed to Surgeon Charles Pritchard in the town of Brecon in 1777 when he was 17 years old for five years. In 1782 at the age of 22 he qualified as a Surgeon and Apothecary[62].

Apart from seeing the residents of the town and the surrounding area he was also the Surgeon at Cardigan Gaol[63] and retained his position as Surgeon and Coroner in the town and county of Breconshire until at least 1798.[64]

John and Eliza Williams had twenty four children, however only sixteen appear in the Baptismal Records at Cenarth. Two others are known from other records. They were all taught at home by their mother. Alban and Robert went on to the Queen Elizabeth School in Carmarthen, before serving apprenticeships and entering the Royal Navy as Surgeons. Owen, John, Stephen, Richard and others whose names we do not know may have entered the Royal Navy at a young age as was common during the Napoleonic Wars. What is certain is that they lost their lives serving their Country.

Of the eight Williams sisters who married, four remained in South Wales while the other four settled in Caernarvonshire, London and Sussex. All of the known Williams children are listed on the next page. They are listed in the order in which they appear in the Cenarth Church Baptismal Registers:- Those who do not appear in these Registers, but are known from other sources, are entered chronologically.

---

61    *Cenarth Church Registers* at Carmarthenshire Record Office
62    Eighteenth Century Medics, P. J. & R. V. Wallis, Newcastle on Tyne, 1988, 2nd Ed. pp 652-3
63    *Ceredigion, Journal of the Cardiganshire Antiquarian Society*, Vol V1/1 1968. Article by A. E. Davies.
64    Universal British Directory, 1793-98, 'Brecon, Williams, John, (F), Surgeon and one of the Coroners of the County.'

*The children of John and Eliza Williams who appear in the Cenarth Church Register and ones known from other sources\*.*

1.  Marg. (or Mary) Williams bapt. Cenarth 21st Sept. 1783.
2.  *Margarette Eleanora (Marella) born 1784.
3.  Owen Williams bapt. Cenarth 28th March 1785.
4.  John Williams bapt. Cenarth 19th July 1786.
5.  Alban Thomas Williams bapt. Cenarth 4th April 1787.
6.  Anna Eliza Williams bapt. Cenarth 29th July 1788.
7.  Louisa Williams bapt. Cenarth 1789.
8.  Robert Williams, bapt. Cenarth 17th Sept. 1791.
9.  Richard Williams bapt. Cenarth 4th Nov. 1792.
10. *Bridget Williams born 1793.
11. Susannah (Susan) Williams bapt. Cenarth 20th April 1795.
12. Jane Williams bapt. Cenarth 17th April 1796.
13. Richard Williams bapt. Cenarth 5th may 1797.
14. Sarah Williams bapt. Cenarth April 1798.
15. Stephen Williams bapt. Cenarth 21st April 1799.
16. Lettice (Letty, Letitia) Williams bapt. Cenarth 19th July 1800.
17. Elizabeth Williams bapt. Cenarth 4th Feb. 1803
18. Grace Williams bapt. Cenarth 26th August 1805.

As this book is about the Beynon/Heslop duel, attention will be focussed on the daughter who inherited the duel bullet from John Williams, and handed it down to subsequent generations. This will be dealt with after a short account of Leticia Williams and her marriage to the famous Revd. John Griffiths, which is relevant to Newcastle Emlyn[65] and its neighbourhood. 'He was another product of the evangelical heartland, being born in Llandyfriog near Newcastle Emlyn .' He was a Curate in his twenties when he was appointed to the Chapel of Ease at Newcastle Emlyn.

Leticia and John Griffiths were married at Cenarth on 13th October 1830. In the same year he was appointed Vicar of Llangeler, which is about four miles from Newcastle Emlyn. A daughter named Anna Maria was born about 1834 in Newcastle Emlyn. Sadly her mother died in 1860. Anna Maria married Thomas Nicholas Gent of Llandilofawr in 1861.

In April 1853 the Revd. Vicar moved to Llandilofawr, Carmarthenshire. His fame was to spread far and wide as vast crowds

65  *The Welsh Evangelists*, Roger L. Brown, Tair Eglwys Press, Tongwynlais, Cardiff, 1986

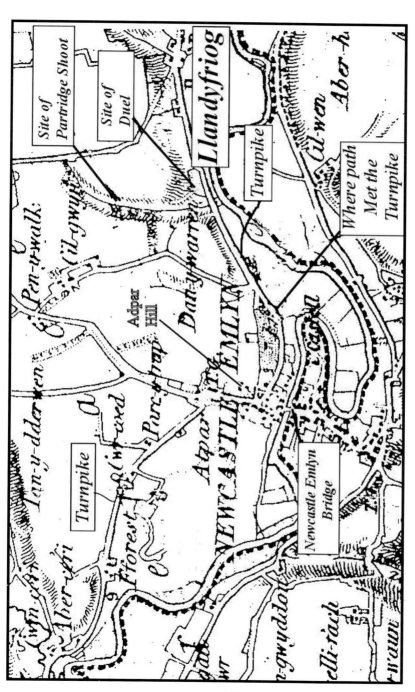

Fig 1.–Location Map showing Adpar Hill; Adpar; Newcastle Emlyn; Danwarren Dingle and Llandyfriog.

Fig 2–Adpar Hill, Adpar. The residence of John Beynon, Attorney at Law.
From a painting in the National Monuments Record of Wales, R.C.A.H.M.W., Aberystwyth. © R.C.A.H.M.W.
Artist is not known but could possibly be Charlotte Louisa Traherne, an amateur artist of 1830-1840's.

*Fig 3–A drawing of the Old Salutation Inn and the bridge at Adpar by Thomas Rowlandson, 1797.*
*© National Library of Wales, Aberystwyth.*

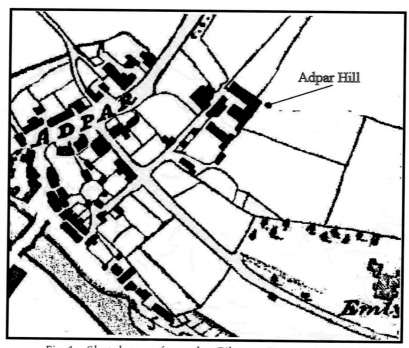

Fig 4a–Sketch map from the Cilgwyn Papers circa 1842
showing the location of Adpar Hill, John Beynon's residence.

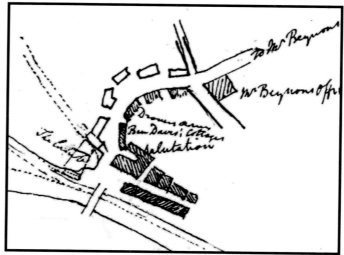

Fig 4b–Sketch map from the Cilgwyn Papers circa 1832
showing the location of the Old Salutation Inn at Adpar.

*Fig 5a–Danwarren Dingle :*
*Where the partridge shoot took place on Thursday 8th September 1814.*

*Fig 5b–Danwarren Dingle :*
*Where the duel took place on Saturday 10th September 1814.*

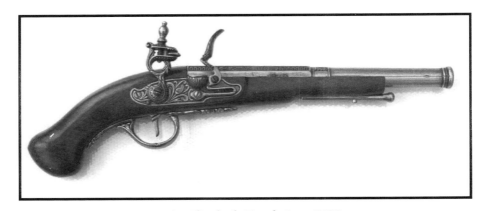

*Fig 6a–Flintlock Pistol circa 1780.*

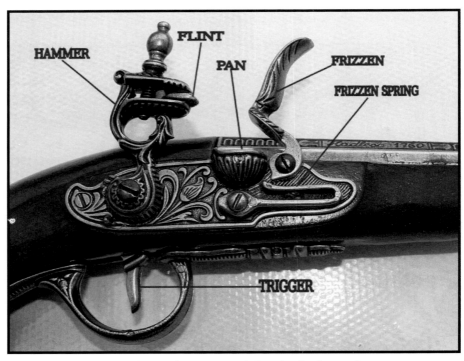

*Fig 6b–Working parts of the Flintlock Pistol*

*Fig 7–Newcastle Emlyn Bridge from a drawing by Thomas Rowlandson circa 1797.*
*© National Library of Wales, Aberystwyth.*

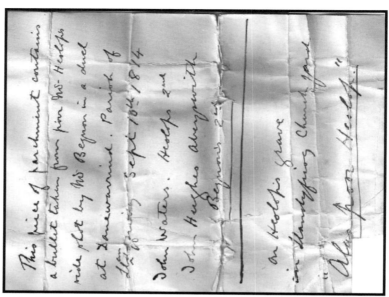

*Fig 8b–Covering note wrapped with the bullet and parchment.*
*Photo: Caty Durham.*

*Fig 8a–The bullet that killed Thomas Heslop.*
*Kept by the Surgeon John Williams and passed down*
*through the Pridham family. It now resides in Oxfordshire.*

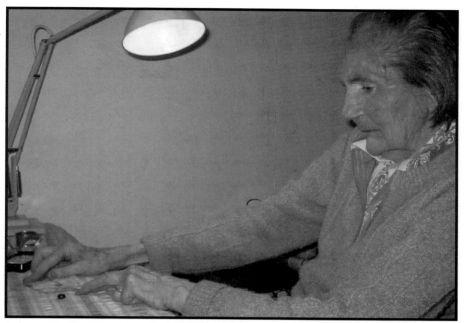

*Fig 9a–Mrs Mary Rose Morris, the present keeper of the bullet.*
*Photo: Caty Durham.*

*Fig 9b–Mrs Jenny F. Pridham*
*(Aunt Jenny),*
*who kept the bullet*
*and wrote the letter regarding it*
*to the Carmarthenshire*
*Antiquarian Society.*
*Photo: Pridham Family Collection.*

*Fig 10a–Llandyfriog Church and churchyard, Ceredigion.*

*Fig 10b–Thomas Heslop's grave in Llandyfriog churchyard.*

Fig 11a–The worn headstone on Thomas Heslop's grave.

Fig 11b–The entry for Thomas Heslop
in the Llandyfriog Church Burial Register.

*Fig 12–Holy Trinity Church Newcastle Emlyn before the rebuilding in 1926. It is possible that the railings at the east end of the church did enclose the Beynon graves.*

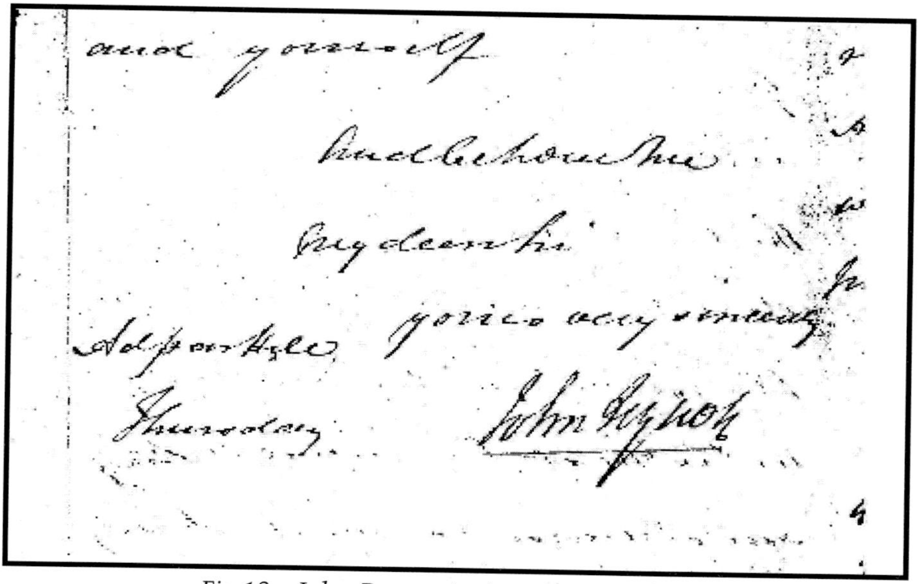

*Fig 13a–John Beynon's signature on a letter*

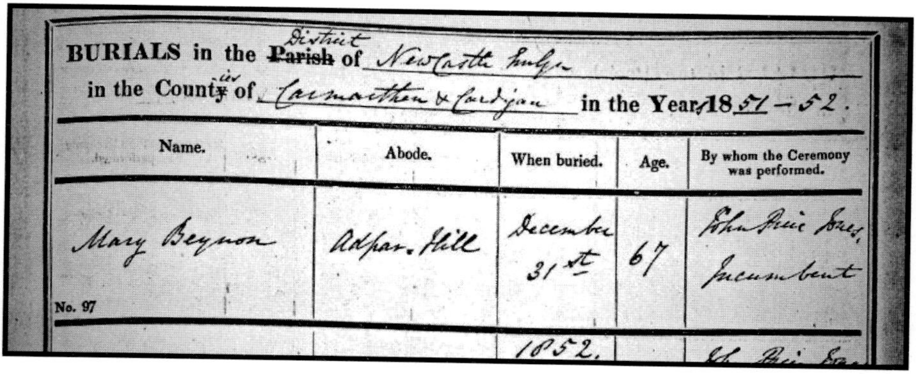

BURIALS in the ~~Parish~~ District of *Newcastle Emlyn*
in the County ~~of~~ in of *Carmarthen & Cardigan* in the Year 18 *51 – 52*

| Name. | Abode. | When buried. | Age. | By whom the Ceremony was performed. |
|---|---|---|---|---|
| Mary Beynon No. 97 | Adpar. Hill | December 31st | 67 | John Price Jones, Incumbent |
| | | 1852. | | Jh. Price Jon |

*Fig 13b–Burial Records for Mary & John Beynon*
*in the Holy Trinity Church Register.*

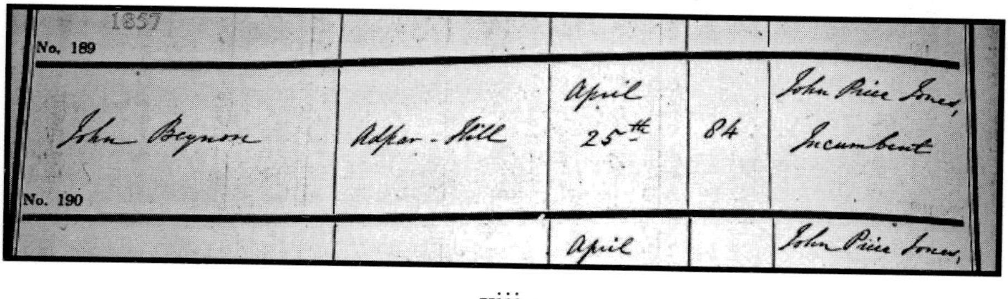

| No. 189 | 1857 | | | | |
|---|---|---|---|---|---|
| John Beynon No. 190 | Adpar. Hill | April 25th | 84 | John Price Jones, Incumbent |
| | | April | | John Price Jones, |

*Fig 14a–Cethin, Llangynin, the birthplace of John Beynon.*

*Fig 14b–Beynon family graves in Llangynin churchyard.*

*Fig 15a–Llwynderw, Pentrecourt where John Beynon and his sister grew up.*

*Fig 15b–Troedrhiwffenyd, Gorrig, Llandysul, another of John Beynon's abodes.*

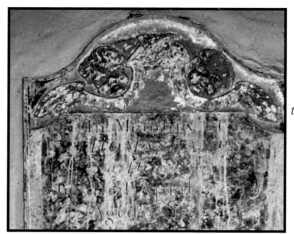

*Fig 16a–Memorial Tablet to 35 year old Thomas James of Henfryn, in Llangeler Parish Church vestry, dated 1794.*

*Fig 16b–Brass Memorial to the Rev. John Griffiths, D.D. at Llandeilo Parish Church.*

flocked to hear him preach. 'Griffiths was widely regarded as one of the great Welsh preachers of his day, some even describing him as the Welsh 'Chrysostom' (silver tongued). His eloquence received the unusual reward of the Lambeth Degree of Doctor of Divinity, awarded him by Archbishop Tait...'

Anna Maria and Thomas Nicholas had two sons: John William Nicholas born in 1862; and Thomas Howells Nicholas born in 1864. It seems that the younger brother only lived for a few years and died in 1874.

John William Nicholas married Kate Ley Driberg in 1892 and they had a daughter Kathleen Mary Nicholas in 1893. Most significant is the fact that Katherine herself had a daughter – Bobby Lewis – who works in the same Church in Llandeilo today where her Great-grandfather was Vicar all those years ago!

There is a memorial to Rev John Griffiths in the Parish Church of St. Teilo in Llandeilo. It is brass mounted in slate. It reads: 'Sacred to the memory of the Rev John Griffiths D.D., formerly Vicar of Llangeler in this county, Vicar of this parish for upwards of 25 years; Rural Dean and Proctor in Convocation. He departed this life Feb 23rd 1878 in his 73rd year. This tablet was erected by his friends. He was a burning and a shining light. John 5: 35'. (In Welsh): 'A'r rhai a droant lawer i gyfiawnder, a fyddant fel y sêr byth yn dragywydd'. Dan. XII, 3. Translated, it says, 'And they that turn many to righteousness shall be as the stars for ever and ever'.

Leticia's elder sister Anna Eliza married Chemist Edward Pridham at Cenarth on 2nd December 1809. They were my Gt-gt-gt-grandparents. It is believed that they lived directly opposite Surgeon John and Anna Eliza Williams in Bridge Street, Newcastle Emlyn; and that Edward's Chemist Shop was close to John's Surgery.

Edward's father, Thomas Collins Pridham 1st (1763-1824) was also a Chemist and was born and grew up in Bideford, Devon. In 1787, upon completion of his apprenticeship he married Ann Powe in Bideford. They moved to Carmarthen almost immediately and Thomas went into business as a Chemist.

John Williams died in 1825 at the age of 65, and his wife Anna Eliza in 1836. Seven of her daughters married and 'bid fair to make the surgeon's widow the grandmother of a colony'.

# The Pridhams in Newcastle Emlyn

The duel of 1814 passed into folklore. The bullet, however, was kept as a memento at the home of the Pridhams in Bridge Street, Newcastle Emlyn. It has remained in the hands of the Pridhams ever since. The eldest son of Edward and Anna Eliza Pridham, Chemist Thomas Collins Pridham 2nd, almost certainly inherited it and took it to his home in Llanelli after his mother's death in 1853. Aunt Jennie (Frances Jane Pridham) lived at the Pridham home in Newcastle Emlyn until 1861 when she married her cousin Albert Edward Pridham. He was a Chemist in Llanelly and he would have inherited the bullet from his father Thomas Collins Pridham 2nd after he died in 1875. After Albert Edward's death in 1882 the bullet naturally remained with his wife, Aunt Jennie. This must have been when it 'was in my possession for some years' as stated in her famous letter[66]. It left Wales with her when she moved to Bath and later Weston-super-Mare. At some stage during this time she may have given it to her husband's only brother Dr. John Williams Pridham who had married and started a medical practice near Weymouth. It then passed to his eldest son Dr. John Alexander Pridham and then to his eldest daughter Mary Rose Morris, and that is where it remains.

The Pridham family needs to be looked at more closely to show how all these family members fit into the picture. Aunt Jennie's father was John Pridham – a younger brother of Thomas Collins Pridham 2nd. John Pridham was born in 1815 and met and married Elizabeth McCarthy in London in 1836. Their first daughter, Anna Eliza Pridham 3rd, was born there in 1838. The family then moved back to Newcastle Emlyn. Elizabeth gave birth to Frances Jane (Aunt Jenny) in 1839; however, she did not recover from the birth and died soon afterwards. She was 25 years old. John was, of course, distraught, and things were to get worse the next year.

In 1840 his sister Anna Eliza Pridham 2nd died of consumption aged 27. A year later his younger brother William Edward, probably also suffering from consumption died aged 17. John Pridham seems to have suffered some kind of breakdown under all this strain, and departed permanently for North America in 1841, leaving his two infant daughters, Anna (Eliza) and Frances (Jane) in the care of his parents, Edward and Anna Eliza and their two remaining daughters Frances Amelia and Mary Bridget.

---

66  Appendix 6. See letter from Frances Jane Pridham to Carmarthenshire Antiquarian Society

The members of the Pridham family in Newcastle Emlyn are listed below as they appear in the 1841 Census for the Parish of Cenarth, Hamlet of Emlyn, Bridge Street.

*Edward Pridham, 50, Druggist; Anna (Eliza) Pridham, 50, Druggist; Frances (Amelia) Pridham, 20, Druggist; Mary (Bridget) Pridham, 15, Druggist; William (Edward) Pridham, 15, Druggist; Anna (Eliza) Pridham, 4; Frances (Jane) Pridham (Aunt Jennie) 18 months.*

Aunt Jennie spent her childhood in the home of her grandparents. Many years later she wrote 'that' letter[67] which recalled that she had "gathered primroses" in the field where the Beynon-Heslop duel had taken place. She also remembered John Beynon as a 'tall very old gentleman'. In one of her last letters to my grandfather she recorded her mistrust of Beynon[68] but as a child her impression of him was merely one of awe.

Her grandfather Edward Pridham died in 1847 and her Grandmother Anna Eliza in 1852. Jennie was a teenager by then and her Aunt Mary Bridget Pridham had to be a parent and teacher to Jennie as well as working as Chemist, Grocer & Stationer in the family shop in Newcastle Emlyn.

There were only two Pridhams in Newcastle Emlyn after 1852 because Frances Amelia had married Chemist Thomas Evans in 1847, and moved to Aberdare. Anna Eliza Pridham 3rd went to live with them, but sadly she died at the age of 22 in 1861.

Jennie had now lost both parents, grandparents, and her only sibling. Jennie's cousin Albert Edward Pridham was still grieving for his mother when his father started a new family. He and his second wife Sarah had two children by the time Jennie's sister, Anna Eliza died. Jennie and Albert Edward must have felt drawn to one another in their suffering.

Marriage between first cousins was accepted in those days and they were married on 30th April 1861 at St. Elvan's Church in Aberdare, just three months after the death of her sister.

In the Census of 1861 we see another profound change at the familiar address in Bridge Street Newcastle Emlyn. Mary Bridget was still running the Grocery shop and had married Daniel Davies. They had three sons:

---

67    Appendix 6. See letter from Frances Jane Pridham to Carmarthenshire Antiquarian Society

68    'I must add that in spite of all the Country "Bucks" say Beynon was a bad lot altho' a gentleman.' Quote from letter dated Jan. 1824 *(Pridham Collection)*

William Edward, David Walter and Francis. In 1891 the parents were still in Newcastle Emlyn, however there was now another Chemist in the family: youngest son Francis is listed as 'Chemist and Druggist' at the same address. This is a return to the profession of his Grandfather Edward Pridham, and it seems that he worked from the very same premises, after four decades!

Twenty years after their wedding Jennie and Edward Albert Pridham were living at 5 Bridge Street Llanelly. They had four children: Frederick; Fanny Rose; Charles; and Herbert. She and Edward Albert had just celebrated their silver wedding anniversary in 1882 when he died at the age of 45.

Her daughter Fanny Rose married Bank Manager Albert Edward Old at Llanelly in 1885. Jennie had to endure another death when Fanny Rose died in 1886 on the day before her first wedding anniversary, and shortly after giving birth to their daughter Gwladys Noel. Jennie decided to leave Wales, and start life again in Bath.

This decision was influenced by the fact that John Williams Pridham, who was her brother-in-law and at the same time her first cousin, lost his wife Alexina at the age of 44 in 1883. They had together planned and built 'Hillfield House' with Surgery attached, at Broadway near Weymouth. Jennie could visit and I think that Jennie would probably have given 'the bullet' to him at around this time, as I do not think that it was something that she would have liked to keep.

Eventually Alexina's nieces, Dilly and Elma, came to keep house for him. After several years he and Elma fell in love. She was more than twenty years his junior, they married in Bergen, Norway in 1890. Dilly and her sister Dolly continued to live with them. John died in 1899 after less than a decade of marriage. However, he and Elma had four sons: my Grandfather, John Alexander; Alban Gerard; Hubert Llewellyn; and Hugh Trevor.

From 1882-1891 Jennie lived in Bath and ran an art needlework and embroidery shop in the most gracious Street in the city – Milsom Street. Mary Alice Wilmot was her 'Assistant' and she married Jennie's youngest son Herbert Thomas Pridham. Sadly Herbert died in 1902.

The next address that we have for Jennie is 14 All Saints Road, Weston-super-Mare. She wrote to her nephew Dr J. A. Pridham from there in 1924 to ask if she might identify him as the present custodian of the bullet in the letter to the newspaper. By this time my Grandfather was 33 years old and living with his wife Margaret and three young children at the same house that his father had built, Hillfield House in Weymouth.

Her final address was in Axebridge where she died in 1930, at the age of 90. Her Granddaughter Gwladys remained close to her right to the end, and took down Jennie's memories. One of her final comments on the early Twentieth Century: ' ...these days of motor maniacs and swank'.

John Alexander Pridham qualified as a medical Doctor at St Bartholomew's Hospital in London, and then served during the Second World War as a Medical Officer with the rank of Captain and eventually Major. He was wounded at the battle of the Somme. Shrapnel from an exploding shell struck the side of his face and he lost his left eye and he was awarded the Military Cross Medal. The following report appeared in the London Gazette in 1918. 'Capt. John Alexander Pridham, R.A.M.C., Spec. Res. For conspicuous gallantry and devotion to duty. He was in charge of. an advanced dressing station where there were a large number of wounded when the enemy attacked. The task of removing the wounded was an extremely difficult one owing to the proximity of the enemy and heavy shell and machine gun fire, but he carried it out successfully, remaining on the spot until all the wounded had been evacuated. By his courage and devotion to duty he was the means of saving many lives'.

After the War he continued his father's medical practice from the surgery at Hillfield House. He married Margaret Smith whom he had met while a medical student in London. They had four daughters: 'Peggy'; Mary Rose; Pauline; and June.

My mother Pauline qualified as a medical Doctor at the Grey's Inn Hospital in London; and this Hospital was hit by a bomb during World War II while she was on duty. She remembers the explosion and then half the passage in which she was standing disappeared, leaving her staring into the open air. She later met my father Tim Crowe while they were working as young doctors at a Hospital in Salisbury, Wiltshire.

After getting married in 1953 they went to Rhodesia, where my father worked as a G.P. and later an E.N.T. Surgeon. My mother's sister June, herself a Nursing sister, and husband Dr. John Wesson also joined us in Rhodesia. Their eldest sister Peggy Pridham also came to live in Africa.

My Grandfather served on the International Organizing Committee which formed The World Medical Association. He served as British

Representative on this Association for some years. I remember him as a wonderfully good-natured Grandfather when he visited us at our home in N'dola, Zambia in 1965. He died on 10th April in the same year but had fulfilled his ambition of getting to know his ten Grandchildren who were born and lived in Africa. There were six of us and my Aunt and Uncle Wesson had four children in Gwanda, Southern Rhodesia. Mary Rose qualified as a Nursing Sister at St. Bartholomew's Hospital. She stayed in England and married Dr Charles Morris of St Bartholomew's Hospital. They had twin sons, Edward and Geoffrey. They have collected and preserved all the family records and that is how Mary Rose Morris came to inherit 'the bullet.'

[I visited Dr. Charles and Mary Rose Morris in Oxfordshire in August 2006 and was fortunate enough and honoured to be able to see and handle the bullet and the pigskin parchment in which it has been wrapped all these years. I am very grateful to them for allowing me this privilege. Ken Jones]

# Chapter 12

# Who Was Who

## John Beynon

John Beynon was born in 1774 the son of William Beynon (d.1781) of Cethin, Llangynin and grandson of John Beynon of Trewern, Llanddewy Velfrey, Whitland. William Beynon's sister Anne married Rev Richard Thomas of Llanfyrnach and lived at Llwynderw, Pentrecourt in the parish of Llangeler. There were no children from this marriage so John Beynon and his sister Elisabeth came to live with Anne and her husband[69]. Anne died in 1796 at the age of 82 and John Beynon inherited Llwynderw. His sister Elisabeth had married Walter Pryce but she died in childbirth.

In 1794 one of John Beynon's neighbours, 35 year old Thomas James of Henfryn, Pentrecwrt in the Parish of Llangeler, challenged Beynon to a horse race through Llandyssil and said he would beat him. Beynon took up the challenge and they galloped down through the main street of the village on April 3rd. The pace was so furious that James' horse failed to negotiate the turn at the narrow bridge and horse and rider ended up in the river Tivy where they both perished. A by now rather indistinct slate memorial stone[70] to Thomas James and the Henfryn family can be seen on the wall of the vestry in Llangeler Parish Church.

John Beynon became a successful attorney in Newcastle Emlyn and lived at Adpar Hill, referred to as 'an elegant villa,' in Frances Jones' *Historic Cardiganshire Homes and their Families.*

John Beynon was a member of the Conservative club at Carmarthen and during an election in August 1832 the members were lampooned in a 'Descriptive Catalogue.'[71] They were given descriptions and two are quoted here; Rev. Lewis of Dyffryn was, 'A sporting Tory Parson,' and John Beynon's was, 'Least said, soonest mended.'

69  *Hanes Plwyf Llangeler a Phenboyr (History of the Parishes of Llangeler & Penboyr)* 1899, pg 127, Daniel E. Jones
70  *Hanes Plwyf Llangeler a Phenboyr (History of the Parishes of Llangeler & Penboyr)* 1899, pg 131, Daniel E. Jones
71  *Carmarthenshire Antiquarian Society, Transactions, Vol 23, pg 52.*

He was agent for the Cilgwyn[72] estate of E. C. L. Hall (later Fitzwilliams) at Adpar and was also agent for the Bronwydd Estate and was appointed steward[73] of the Baronetcy of Kemmaes in 1817 by Thomas Lloyd of Bronwydd. Beynon was quite capable of indulging in shady practices and to make matters worse, he was paid from 'profits arising out of the Chief Rents, Estrays, Mortuaries and Alienations derivable from the barony.' His methods were infamous within the barony and elsewhere.

He was also a Trustee of the Carmarthen and Newcastle Emlyn Turnpike Trust and was part of the committee appointed to look at the accounts of the Trust, called by Edward Charles Lloyd Hall of Emlyn Cottage, Adpar in June 1843.

He is named as John Beynon Esq., J.P., of Adpar Hill and Ffynon Wervil, Llangrannog in *The Times* of November 23, 1853 a Patron of the planned new Railway from Carmarthen to Cardigan via Newcastle Emlyn.

Beynon married Mary a widow, in 1820[74]. *The Cambrian Index* tells us that she was Mary Russell from Somerset. Francis Jones' *Historic Cardiganshire Homes and their Families* tells us that she was a widow, Mary Lewis, whose husband James died in 1793. Her sister Gwenllian, married William Williams, Blaendyffryn, the Cardiganshire coroner who sat on the body of Thomas Heslop. They were the daughters of the late David and Bridget Davies of Troedrhiwffenydd, [Troedrhiwfynydd], [Troedrhiwpenyd], Gorrig, Llandyssil. John Beynon owned Troedrhiwpenyd and rented it out to Samuel Griffiths.

The 1841 census records John and Mary Beynon and four female servants at Adpar Hill. In 1851 John and Mary Beynon (listed in the census as from Devon) together with six servants lived at Adpar Hill. Mary Beynon died in December 1851, aged 67. This means that she was born in 1784 and would have been nine years old if she was the widow mentioned in the [75]*Cardiganshire Book*. Following John Beynon's death the house was in the hands of William and Jemima Bartlett Wilson Prout[76]. William Prout was an Attorney but is described in the census as 'Landed Proprietor.'

---

72   *Princelings, Privilege & Power, L. Baker-Jones, Gomer, Page 76*
73   *NLW, Bronwydd Papers, 609*
74   *Cambrian Index, 18 March 1820*
75   *Historic Cardiganshire Homes and Their Families*, Major Francis Jones, Brawdy Books, 2000, pg 261
76   According to the 1861 Census she hailed from the Parish of Llandyfriog

John Beynon died of old age and debility in April 1857 aged 84. He and his wife Mary are buried in the Holy Trinity Churchyard in Newcastle Emlyn. In his will John Beynon stipulated that after his death the inheritors of his estate were to 'keep in repair all the stone and ironwork about the said graves and also protect the same with three coats of good oil paint every fifth year at least,' and the same was to apply to the family graves at Llangynin Church where he had also erected substantial iron railings. These railings enclose very tightly the three tombs of some of his ancestors. The names Thomas Beynon, James Beynon, Rees Beynon, Mary Beynon and William Beynon, can still be read. There are no surviving records for the Church before 1813 and those from 1813 onwards are in a sad state.

No trace of the Beynon graves can be found in Holy Trinity churchyard at Newcastle Emlyn. They were possibly moved when the Church was rebuilt in 1926. A photograph of Holy Trinity Church before rebuilding shows a set of railings enclosing graves at the chancel end, which was enlarged at the time of rebuilding.

Beynon left money in his will to his servants and also a suit in which to mourn him. He left an annuity of £300 p.a. to Jemima Bartlett Wilson Prout, not to be managed by her husband. Jemima Bartlett Wilson Prout had been a Leslie of Stradmore, Cardiganshire, before she married William Prout in 1834. His personal estate he left to David Pugh his nephew, of Manorabon [Manoravon], Llandeilo[77]. It was eventually inherited by the Protheroe-Beynons of Trewern, Whitland.

Sometime after John Beynon's death Adpar Hill was acquired by the (Hall), Fitzwilliams family of Cilgwyn. In [78]1873 E. C. L. H. Fitzwilliams lived there. The house was described as a square, three bay, three storey, regency building that stood in a property of 904 acres. Around 1910 it was demolished by Charles Fitzwilliams of Cilgwyn who described it as 'a house not fit for a gentleman to live in.'

77    John Beynon's Will
78    *Historic Cardiganshire Homes & Their Families*, Major Francis Jones, Brawdy Books, 2000, pg 14

*An extract from Cardiganshire Quarter Sessions Wednesday 19th October 1814 held at Lampeterpontsteffan[sic] Town Hall.* [79]

Be it remembered that the appointment of John Beynon, gent., as Clerk of the Peace of this County in the room of Herbert Lloyd, gent., deceased was read and filed and that the said John Beynon did in open court take the oath required to be taken by the Clerk of the Peace before he enters upon the execution of his office according to the statute in such case made and provided.

*And,*

Ordered that John Beynon of Troedrhiwfenyd in this County, gent., be appointed Solicitor for the County[80] in the room of the late Herbert Lloyd, gent., deceased and he is accordingly appointed Solicitor for this County with the usual salary.

## James Hughes.

Beynon's 'second,' James Hughes, was from Aberystwith. He worked for Beynon at Newcastle Emlyn.

James married Mary, youngest daughter of Sir Thomas Bonsall of Fronfraith, Llanbadarn Fawr, on 18 February 1820. A daughter was born in March 1821 and a son in March 1822. Their home was at Glanrheidol, a residence near Capel Bangor, Llanbadarn, Aberystwith. This had been bequeathed to his wife Mary and when they took it over in 1824[81] he changed his name to James Hughes-Bonsall. He was a founder of a firm of solicitors in Aberystwith and was also a Mayor of that town. James Hughes died on 13th June 1858 aged 70 at Glanrheidol.

*Cardiganshire Quarter Sessions Wednesday 19th October 1814 held at Lampeterpontsteffan Town Hall.*

Ordered that James Hughes[82] of Aberystwith in this County, gent., be appointed Treasurer of the County Stock of this County in the room of John Beynon who has been appointed Clerk of the Peace.

79   Ceredigion Archives, Aberystwyth. Quarter Session Records for Cardiganshire, pg 310

80   Ceredigion Archives, Aberystwyth. Quarter Session Records for Cardiganshire, pg 314

81   *NLW*, Llidiardau Estate Records, C18-C20

82   Ceredigion Archives, Aberystwyth. Quarter Session Records for Cardiganshire, pg 310

# John Walters (Heslop's second)

In 1804, Aberglasney was sold by William Herbert Dyer to Thomas Phillips for 10,000 guineas. He had seen service in India as a surgeon with the East Indies Company. Thomas's sister, Bridget married Abel Walters of Perthcereint [Beddgeraint] Bettws Ifan, in the parish of Penbryn, Cardiganshire in 1780. John Walters was Abel Walters' son and lived with his unmarried sisters, Jane and Frances in Newcastle Emlyn where he practised as an attorney.

John Walters succeeded to Aberglasney when his uncle Thomas Phillips, the purchaser of Aberglasney, died in 1824. John Walters added the surname Phillips to his name by Royal Licence in 1825[83], a condition on succeeding to the estate, and became known as John Walters-Phillips. He married Anne Bowen, fourth daughter of Thomas Bowen of Waunifor in 1817. John and Anne's daughter, Mary Anne, married John Pugh Vaughan Pugh of Bwlchbychan, Cardiganshire. Their son Thomas died in infancy. There were two other daughters, Bridget Jane who married Cecil Anson Harries, and Elizabeth Frances, who married Frederick Lewis Lloyd Philipps.

When Thomas Philipps lived at Aberglasney he was a Justice of the Peace, and served as High Sheriff of Carmarthenshire in 1813; his nephew, John Walters-Phillips, acted as his deputy. At Carmarthen Assizes in August 1816, Thomas Philipps brought a case[84] against a Mr Richards, a publican of Llangathen. Richards was accused of sending a message to Philipps in the nature of a provocation to fight a duel. After the case had been put by the counsel the learned judge in his summing up directed the jury to acquit the dedfendant. John Walters-Philipps became a magistrate himself and also served as High Sheriff of Carmarthenshire in 1841.

We do not know much about Rees Thomas or George Phillips who were at the dinner at Beynon's house on the 8th September 1814. It is possible that they were both attorneys living in Carmarthen.

There was a **Rees Thomas** who was an attorney of Egremont House, Carmarthen who died in March 1834 and also a **George Phillips** another Carmarthen attorney, who married Miss Hughes of Tregib, nr Llandilo in 1813.

---

83    See Appendix 6 and *Cambrian Index*, 26 March 1825
84    Cambrian Index, 17 August 1816

# Serjeant Samuel Heywood

Serjeant Samuel Heywood was the judge who tried Beynon, Hughes and Walters at Cardigan in 1815. He was a judge and author; he was born on the 8 October 1753 at Liverpool. He was educated at the dissenting academy at Warrington, and subsequently at Trinity Hall, Cambridge. Not liking the Anglican worship he absented himself from services and did not take a degree.

Making the law his career, he studied at the Inner Temple, was called to the bar in 1778, and became a Serjeant-at-law in 1794. He practised extensively on the northern circuit, and became Chief Justice of Wales and a judge of the Carmarthen circuit in 1807 which included Haverfordwest and Cardigan.

He already enjoyed the reputation of being an expert on electoral law, publishing *Digest of the Law Concerning County Elections* in 1790 and *Digest of the Law Respecting Borough Elections* in 1797. He had also published a pamphlet entitled, *The Right of Protestant Dissenters to a complete Toleration asserted*, in 1788.

Judge Samuel Heywood sat in judgment on the trial of Evan Davies, the case following the Beynon trial, one of burglary, at the Old Salutation Tavern, Adpar, Newcastle Emlyn. He passed the death sentence on Evan Davies,[85] but Davies was later reprieved.

Samuel Heywood did, however, sentence 29 year old William James from Pennant near Llanon in Cardiganshire to death for breaking into a house with an axe, terrorising the occupants and making off with two pocket books' worth 5 shillings, one pair of scales worth 5 shillings, a Sovereign and 46 promissory notes to the vale of £101.

He spent three months in gaol until his trial on 17th September 1821, and having made three attempts to escape he was placed in irons. For fixing the irons Humphrey Morris of Cardigan was paid £1/5/6. According to the *Cambrian* he was hanged at Cardigan on the 15th of October 1821, in the presence of a large crowd of people. For supplying the timber and erecting and taking down the gallows Thomas Oliver, a carpenter of Cardigan, received £8/5/-.

---

85  See Appendix 10 and *NLW, Crime and Punishment* File No 4/912/3 Document No 57

The *Cambrian* reported on the 6th September 1828 that 78 year old Mr Justice Heywood had an attack of paralysis, possibly a heart attack when at Haverfordwest the previous Friday morning. He was preparing to leave for Carmarthen where he was expected to have opened the Commission on the same day. The Mayor and other Officers of the Corporation of Carmarthen, together with William Chambers Esq., the High Sheriff, proceeded to the Town Hall where the sudden illness of the learned judge was formally announced, to the great dismay of many suitors and witnesses who were in attendance from different parts of the County. The Court was adjourned *sine die;* the *Cambrian* further informed its readers on 13th September 1828 that the learned Judge had expired at Tenby on the 11th September. Since his attack of paralysis at Haverfordwest, little hopes had been entertained of his recovery.

The *Cambrian* in its obituary for Serjeant Heywood said, 'Throughout a long life, and in a profession said to be not remarkably favourable to the purity of the political character, Mr Heywood was inflexibly honest and consistent; and in private life he attracted the esteem and attachment of a numerous circle of friends by the sincerity and kindness of his heart and manners.'

The *Carmarthen Journal* of September 19 1828 reported that the body of the late Serjeant Heywood had arrived at Carmarthen from Tenby on Monday and had rested for the night at the Ivy Bush Inn on its way to Bristol for internment.

On Tuesday morning the hearse and attendants proceeded on their route for Swansea and the mournful cavalcade was escorted by the Mayor and Corporation in their robes, sword of state, mace etc., enveloped in black crepe. The County and Borough gaolers preceded the cortege with black wands. Judge Serjeant Samuel Heywood was obviously held in high esteem by the people of Carmarthen for a large body of respectable inhabitants in mourning turned out and accompanied his corpse as far as the Borough boundary, the bells of St Peters tolling the funeral peal.

## Coroner William Williams

William Williams, lived at Blaendyffryn, Parish of Bangor Teifi, near Llandyssil [Llandysul]. According to Francis Jones' *Historic Cardiganshire Homes and their Families*, Blaendyffryn had been the home of three High Sheriffs. He was one of the Cardiganshire coroners and sat on the body of

Thomas Heslop at the inquest held at the Salutation Tavern on the afternoon of the duel.

The inquests he had sat on, for the period from the duel to the time of the Beynon trial, were listed in the Quarter Sessions of April 5th 1815, when the Treasurer of the County Stock was ordered to pay his bill of £13/14/3d in full. They were mostly inquests on children; a pot of boiling whey toppled on a two year old; a cart hub leaning on a hedge fell on a four year old; three infants playing together in a kitchen when the clothes of one of them caught fire and he burned to death; a pot of boiling water taken off the fire and a four year old fell backwards into it; a three year old fell face first into the fire and lived for thirteen days, and a man found drowned and suffocated at Llanina. It has been stated elsewhere that John Beynon drew up William Williams' will, and was a beneficiary, as was Surgeon John Williams.

# *Appendix 1*

National Library of Wales, Crime and Punishment
File No 4/912/3 Document No 47

## INQUEST REPORT ON THOMAS HESLOP
### 10th SEPTEMBER 1814

An Inquisition indented take for our Lord the King at the Parish of Llandyfriog in the County of Cardigan the Tenth of September in the 54th year of the reign of our Sovereign Lord George III by the Grace of God of the United Kingdom and Ireland, King, Defender of the faith and so forth, before William Williams one of the Coroners of our said Lord the King for the said County.

On view of the body of Thomas Heslop Esquire, then and there lying dead, upon the oath of Lewis Price, John Enoch, Joshua Jones, Richard Jones, David Evans, Thomas Jones, Enoch Williams, David Jones, Benjamin Davies, Philip Protheroe, James Griffiths, Evan Evans, John Francis and John Richards, good and lawful men of the said County duly chosen, and who being then and there duly sworn and charged to inquire for our said Lord and King, when how and by what means, the said Thomas Heslop came to his death do upon their oath say that the said Thomas Heslop on the Tenth day of September in the year aforesaid at Blaenant dingle at the Parish and in the County aforesaid and found dead with a leaden ball shot out of a certain pistol, charged and loaded with gunpowder and leaden bullet by some person unknown, almost through the breast of him the said Thomas Heslop which he the person unknown then and there had and held in his right hand, to and against the right side of him the said Thomas Heslop did then and there shoot off and discharge by means whereof. He the said person unknown, wilfully and of his own malice forethought did then and there give unto him the said Thomas Heslop with the leaden bullet aforesaid, so as aforesaid, shot off and discharged out of the pistol aforesaid by the force of the gunpowder aforesaid in and upon the right side of him the aforesaid Thomas Heslop, one mortal wound penetrating the right side of him the aforesaid Thomas Heslop, of which said mortal wound he, the said Thomas Heslop then and there instantly died, and so the Jurors aforesaid upon their oath aforesaid Do say that the said person unknown, him the said Thomas Heslop in manner and means aforesaid, feloniously, wilfuly, and of his malice aforethought, did kill and murder against the Peace of our said Lord the King, his Crown and Dignity – In witness whereof as well the said Coroner, Jurors aforesaid have to this inquisition set their hands and seals, the day, year and place above mentioned.

Signed by: *William Williams and Lewis Price, John Enoch, Joshua Jones, Richard Jones, David Evans, Thomas H. Jones (his mark), Enoch Williams, David Jones, Benjamin Davies, Philip Protheroe, James Griffiths (his mark), Evan Evans, John Francis and John Richards.*

# *Appendix 2*

*National Library of Wales, Crime and Punishment
File No 4/912/3 Document No 5*

## THE GREAT SESSIONS OF CARDIGANSHIRE, 22nd MARCH 1815
### THE INDICTMENT OF JOHN BEYNON, JOHN WALTERS & JAMES HUGHES

**INDICTMENT** has been changed to reduce the charge from murder to manslaughter. Strikethroughs initialled by **W.O.** – *William Owen (Attorney General for the Carmarthen circuit)*. On the front of the Indictment the words, **'True bill for manslaughter'** have been crossed out.

Cardiganshire to wit. The Jurors for our Lord the King upon their oath present that John Beynon late of the Parish of Llandyfriog in the County of Cardigan, Gentleman, John Walters late of the same gentleman and James Hughes late of the same gentleman.

[Not having the fear of God before their eyes but being moved and seduced by the instigation of the Devil] on the tenth day of September in the 54th year of the reign of our Sovereign Lord George III by the Grace of God of the United Kingdom and Ireland, King Defender of the Faith with force and so forth at the Parish aforesaid in the County aforesaid in and upon Thomas Heslop in the peace of God and our said Lord the King then and there being feloniously and wilfuly **W.O.** [and of their malice aforethought] did make an assault and that the said John Beynon a certain pistol of the value of 5 shillings then and there loaded and charged with gunpowder and one leaden bullet which he the said John Beynon in his right hand then and there had and held so against and upon the said Thomas Heslop then and there feloniously and wilfuly W.O. [and of his malice aforethought] did shoot and discharge and that the said John Beynon with the leaden bullet aforesaid out of the pistol aforesaid then and there by force of the gunpowder shot and sent forth as aforesaid the said Thomas Heslop in and upon the right side of him the said Thomas Heslop near the right pap of him the said Thomas Heslop then and there feloniously and wilfuly W.O. [and of his malice aforethought] and strike penetrate and wound giving to the said Thomas Heslop then and there with the leaden bullet aforesaid, so aforesaid discharged and shot off of the pistol aforesaid by the said John Beynon in and upon the right side of him the said Thomas Heslop near the right pap of him the said Thomas Heslop one mortal wound of the depth of six inches and of the breadth of one inch of which said mortal wound the said Thomas Heslop then and there instantly died and that the aforesaid John Walters and James Hughes then and there feloniously and willingly **W.O.** [of their malice aforethought] were present aiding, helping, abetting and comforting assisting and maintaining the said John Beynon the felony of **W.O.** [murder] aforesaid in manner and form aforesaid to do and commit, and so the Jurors aforesaid upon their oath aforesaid do say that the said John Beynon, John Walters and James Hughes the said Thomas Heslop then and there in manner and form aforesaid feloniously, wilfully **W.O.** [and of their malice aforethought] did kill **W.O.** [and murder] against the peace of our said Lord, the King, his crown and dignity.

Signed **Wm. Owen.**

(William Owen was the Attorney General for the Carmarthen Circuit which included Carmarthen, Haverfordwest and Cardigan.)

# *Appendix 3*

*National Library of Wales, Crime and Punishment*
*File No 4/912/3 Document No 4*

## LIST OF JURORS AT JOHN BEYNON, JAMES HUGHES, JOHN WALTERS' TRIAL

Printed List of 59 Jurors 12 marked with **S = Selected**

| | | | |
|---|---|---|---|
| 1 | William Davies | Maesdwyfrwd, Llanwnen | |
| 2 | Morgan Evans | Llansantfraed | |
| 3 | William Griffith | Llanrhystid | |
| 4 | John Morgan | Glanywern, Llanfihangel Ystrad | |
| 5 | Abraham Davies | Gwerniad, Llangoedmore | |
| 6 | William Phillips | Cardigan | |
| 7 | Richard Jones | Llanbadarn-Trefeglwys | |
| 8 | David James | Goitre, Llangunfelyn | |
| 9 | David Davies | Llain, Brongwyn | |
| 10 | David Evans | Olmarch, Bettws Leicky | S |
| 11 | Richard James | Crwngwenog, Cynillmawr | |
| 12 | Peter Davies | Glyn, Llanio | |
| 13 | David Jones | Penrallt, Llandissiliogogo | S |
| 14 | Daniel Evans | Parkey, Llangeitho | S |
| 15 | Thomas William | Blaenllyn, Cardigan | |
| 16 | Jenkyn Beynon | Pennar, Lladissiliogogo | S |
| 17 | James James | Cringa, Llandygwydd | |
| 18 | Evan Davies | New Inn, Llanfihangel Ystrad | |
| 19 | Evan James | Pantgwyn, Llandyssil | S |
| 20 | Morgan Pugh | Llanddewy-Aberarth | |
| 21 | David Thomas | Henfedde, Lampeter | |
| 22 | David Morgan | Tynycae, Cynillmawr | S |
| 23 | Joshua Davies | Blaenbedw-isaf, Llandissiliogogo | |
| 24 | William Julia | Aberystwyth | |
| 25 | Evan Lewis | Penrallt, Llangrannog | S |
| 26 | Evan Evans | Gorrig Inn, Llandyssil | |
| 27 | Richard Thomas | Gwarcwm, Parcilcanol | |
| 28 | William Davies | Angel, Cardigan | S |
| 29 | Jenkin Jones | Caehaidd, Henfynyw | |

| 30 | Evan Morgan | Perthgwennin, Llansantffraid | |
|----|-------------|------------------------------|---|
| 31 | James Davies | Aberystwyth | |
| 32 | David Phillips | Weegddu, Llanddewy Aberarth | |
| 33 | Walter Morgan | Aberystwyth | |
| 34 | Thomas Griffith | Pennant, Llanfihangel-Trefechan | |
| 35 | Griffith Griffith | Rhydyronen, Ciliau | |
| 36 | David Davies | Goitre, Llanrhystid | |
| 37 | David Evans | Rhydowen, Llandyssil | |
| 38 | John Davies | Cardigan | |
| 39 | David Edwards | Parcel, Garthelly | |
| 40 | David Davies | Blaenywern, Llandissiliogogo | |
| 41 | David Evans | Nantygelli | |
| 42 | Evan David John | Llanbadarn Fawr | |
| 43 | Thomas James | Tynyrhose, Cynnillmawr | |
| 44 | Evan Evans | Penyweeg, Llanllwchairne | |
| 45 | Thomas Jenkins | Rhydybenne, Llanfihangel Ystrad | |
| 46 | Walter Jones | Nantypelle, Llanllwchairne | S |
| 47 | Evan Joseph | Pantyscawen, Llandyssil | S |
| 48 | John Jones | Velinfach, Cefnmaenmawr | S |
| 49 | John Hughes | Llanfairclydoge | |
| 50 | John Jones | Cailan & Maesmawr | |
| 51 | Daniel Evans | Penywalk, Llandefriog | |
| 52 | John Jones | Pendderw, Llandissiliogogo | S |
| 53 | John Mathias | Cardigan | |
| 54 | Evan Evans | Llanrhystid, Haminiog | |
| 55 | David Evans | ———— Sysillt | |
| 56 | John Jones | Tregaron | |
| 57 | John Davies | Penforthy, Bettws Evan | |
| 58 | John Jones | Cefnllech, Llanbadarn Fawr | |
| 59 | John Roderick | Llanfihangel Gene'r Glyn | |

The sum of 40 shillings was mentioned at the bottom of the sheet

# *Appendix 4*

*In the National Library of Wales are some thirty volumes (ADD MSS 193D – 224D) which contain original notes taken by one of the Welsh Circuit Judges – Samuel Heywood – at the Great Sessions of Cardigan – Carmarthenshire and Pembrokeshire from 1807 to 1820.*

*Volume XX1 (212D) for the Autumn Sessions 1814, Cardigan and Spring 1815, Cardigan contains (pp 46 – 55) an account of the trial of John Beynon for killing Thomas Heslop in a duel at Newcastle Emlyn in 1814.*

*The Volume XX1 (212D) regarding the trial was transcribed by George Eyre Evans and published in the Carmarthenshire Antiquarian Society Transactions Volume XV11 Parts XL111, XL1V 1923-1924. Pages 33–36. These Transactions can be found in the Carmarthenshire Archives at Carmarthen.*

## JUDGES NOTES

*This transcript of the Judges Notes is from The Carmarthenshire Antiquarian Transactions by George Eyres Evans. (Also printed in the Antiquarian Column of the Carmarthen Journal) and are printed here in full.*

Prisoners

Rex:      Versus John Beynon
               John Walters
               James Hughes

## Manslaughter

On September 10th Beynon for shooting Thomas Heslop with a leaden bullet discharged from a pistol, John Walters and James Hughes present for abetting and assisting John Beynon in so shooting.

Attorney General and Bligh for prosecution
J. Jones and Morgan for prisoner

Prosecutor - John Heslop

Witnesses    John Williams
                Edward Pridham

Attorney General – Only Witnesses

Only circumstances arise from account they themselves have given to the surgeon.

Glad not obliged to state law upon the subject.

John Williams – a Surgeon at Newcastle Emlyn knew Thomas Heslop in September last (1814) was called in on 10th September. Mr James Hughes called at my house very early in morning when I was dressing and inquired if I was at home. I heard his voice as I was coming down that instant. He requested I would go to certain place in a dingle called Cwm Ganwarrig [*Danwarren*] and to make what haste I could for Mr Heslop was hit or shot, and begged I would take my instruments and other means in my power to render him every assistance I could.

I went on.

Hughes did not go with me.

On the bridge I met Mr John Walters who also desired I would make all the haste I could and he would show me the place where he lay.

Walters went with me part of the way and we met Mr Beynon.

Mr Walters spoke to Mr Beynon: 'My good fellow you had better take yourself off as soon as you can.'

Mr Beynon made no reply but walked on.

Walters went with me to the Turnpike road which led to the spot, and I desired him there to return.

Walters returned to Newcastle Emlyn and I went on to spot where Mr Heslop lay.

I found him.

He was quite dead and cold, lying on his back and on examining cause of death I found a pistol bullet had penetrated his right side, gone through his left side and was loose in his flannel waistcoat.

A number of people collected and the corpse carried to the 'Salutation' at Newcastle Emlyn.

In returning to Newcastle Emlyn met Walters nearly where we parted. 'It is,' said he, 'an unfortunate event, but I could not help it though.' I endeavoured to put a stop to it. Poor Heslop was determined upon it. I pointed out to him the impropriety of the ridiculous demand suggested (?) to have preceded and advised him to fire low; and Mr Heslop said to me (Walters) 'No I will fire high. I will be damned if I will not fire through his heart if I can and afterwards I will have the other scoundrel out.' He did not mention any names.

Had conversation with Beynon after jury had sat on body.

I awaited effect of verdict. I went to acquaint Mr Beynon the event. He thanked me and I retired.

On following Sunday I called on Beynon and had a conversation with him. He said it was an unfortunate accident; he could not avoid it in duty to his character and honour.

'I was compelled to it.' He said he had a written challenge from Mr Heslop.

When we came to the ground it was agreed we should fire the distance of twelve paces, and Mr Hughes should give word of command.

When they came to ground Heslop observed the sun was rather too bright for his eyes on which Mr Beynon said, 'I will give you the choice of ground.'

They did exchange ground.

When the word 'Present' was given they both 'presented', and before the word 'Fire', Heslop said 'Stop.'

On which Mr Beynon recovered his pistol expecting some explanation. Instead of which he deliberately brought his pistol down to level at Mr Beynon's body and said, 'Go on.'

On which word 'Fire' was given. I do not recollect any more.

When Beynon said he expected an explanation, he did expect it, hoped it would be so.

Mr Hughes much affected. Only said, 'Mr. Heslop was shot.'

Beynon in great affliction. Was seen as well as Walters.

Had known Beynon many years, particularly good humoured, never knew him grumble. Can say the same of the two (other) gentlemen.

When pistol aimed at Beynon he brought pistol gradually down deliberately and aimed at his heart.

Hughes told me the pan did not recede but the cock went down.

(This was Heslop's pistol which did not go off, but if it had would probably have hit Beynon's heart.)

Walters – the bullet was occasion of Heslop's death.

Edward Pridham

Set up by Attorney General.

Knew Heslop; sported with him. He said that Heslop said he had a quarrel with Beynon and had sent him a challenge.

I spoke about settling, advised him to be cool.

He answered he would accept no apology unless Mr Beynon would upon his knees and then he would post him on every door as a coward.

I advised him to be cool, but not prevailing, I got up to leave the room and leaving room I requested that he fired low.

His answer was, 'No I will shoot him through the heart, if it is in my power, and then I will call that rascal Hughes out.'

He said no more.

John Beynon, —————
Great and unprovoked insult.
Sought to make amicable terms.
Provocation.
Challenge.
Nothing but my life would satisfy.
Only alternative to be a coward.
September 8th – Friends to dine.
After dinner conversation on sporting.
I changed conversation but afterwards renewed.
He would shoot under window of my garden.
I took hand in mine 'My dear Heslop' civil as I could be etc., etc.
I insisted on quitting house and turned him out.

Next day I received a challenge.

I said I was engaged this day, I would meet him the next. I did this to give an opportunity for tempers to cool and desired James Hughes to make it so.

Pridham had conversation.

No evidence to affect Hughes or Walters.

Rees Thomas,—————
Knew Heslop who had lived at Carmarthen, and Beynon, he had been some time at Newcastle Emlyn.

On 8th September dined with Beynon.

A large Party, Mr Lewis of Dyffryn came in.

A conversation upon sporting between deceased and Mr Lewis of Dyffryn, and deceased said he had been out on a day or two before with Mr Williams of Alderbrook Hall and seen a great many birds, partridges, but had very bad sport; only killed a brace or two that season but had shot close to the house of Mr Williams.

Mr Lewis said it was not usual to sport on land of gentlemen with whom not acquainted without introduction.

Heslop said he would shoot but Lewis convinced him.

Lewis on right of Beynon, Heslop on left. Beynon endeavoured to turn the conversation.

George Phillips, Lewis, Heslop, Beynon and myself stayed to supper. Heslop was again on Beynon's left hand.

Mr Hughes, Heslop, Beynon and myself only persons left.

About 1.00 o'clock Heslop entered upon subject again without Beynon introducing it. He said he had very bad sport. Should sport when he pleased. Did not care for Cardigan gentlemen.

Beynon took him by the hand and said, 'My dear Heslop, let the subject drop. It is a very disagreeable one to me and I am satisfied you will think differently in the morning.'

Heslop went on and repeated he would sport where he pleased. He did not care for the Cardiganshire gentlemen. He would shoot when he pleased.

Beynon said he would then spoil his own sport and lose the pleasure he came for.

Heslop very violent.
Beynon very cool.

Beynon said if he was sincere in this he should not be allowed to carry a gun another day in that country.

Heslop said his man Owen (Beynon's man) killed more game than any other man in the country; and he would prevent him [Heslop] from killing game.

Beynon asked if he would take any more wine.

He declined.

Mr Beynon said, 'I wish you a good night.'

He did not take the hint.

Heslop got up then and said he should not go out.

He asked me whether I would be his friend. I declined.

Then appealed to Hughes, who also declined, thinking he had behaved ill.

Heslop then turned round on Beynon and said, with his fist clenched, as a man in a passion, – 'You are a damned villain and scoundrel, and you shall answer for this.' He repeated twice or thrice.

Beynon rang the bell and ordered his servant to conduct Heslop out of the house. Servant laid hold of arm and led him out.

Proved handwriting of Thomas Heslop. [The challenge]

I slept at Beynon's that night.

Next morning he felt regret not anger.

*Challenge read.*

*Sir John Owen:* Had known Mr Beynon a great number of years, very intimately: particularly good, mild and humane disposition.

*Mr Powell of Nanteos:* Six or seven years; perfectly mild, humane, and excellent character.

*Mr Lewes of Llysnewydd:* Has known Beynon twenty years, remarkably mild, humane gentleman, and cautious and circumspect in every respect.

*Colonel Brigstocke:* Great number of years, particularly mild and good temper. Never observed disposition to quarrel.

*Thomas Lloyd of Bronwydd:* Several years, a great number. As gentlemanly a man in manners as I ever knew.

*Mr Lloyd Williams:* Fourteen years, very gentlemanly, kind and gentle, not the least disposition to quarrel.

*Mr Lewis of Dyffryn:* From a child. Particularly refined, particularly mild and gentle. He got drunk with him very often, never quarrelsome even when drunk.

*Mr Colby:* A good many years, remarkably mild and humane a gentleman. Sober and cautious and circumspect in every respect.

*Captain Brigstocke:* Fourteen or fifteen years. Good tempered, quiet, inoffensive.

*Mr Price:* Many years. Remarkably mild humane gentleman.

*Walters and Hughes:* Not guilty. Beynon – Guilty, fined,

Imprisonment till paid.

# *Appendix 5*

## CRIMINAL REGISTER

*Extra details are to be found in Criminal Registers 1805–92
NLW FILM 854. Page 23 Cardigan Spring Sessions 1815
in microfilmed register.*

| | |
|---|---|
| John Beynon | Guilty of Manslaughter |
| | Imprisoned until fine paid |
| | Fined 1 shilling |
| John Walters | Not Guilty |
| James Hughes | Not Guilty |

# *Appendix 6*

## REFERENCES

In October of 1814 the **Carmarthen Journal** reported that John Beynon Esq., solicitor of Newcastle Emlyn had been appointed by the Lord Lieutenant of Cardigan as Clerk of the Peace for the said County in the room of Herbert Lloyd, Esq., deceased. (That information and the following letter contradicts the theory that John Beynon ran away to America).

### Carmarthenshire Antiquarian Society, Transactions, Vol 12 Page 33.

*(Letter written by Lettice Rogers, sister-in-law of Surgeon John Williams, to one of her sisters).*

Autumn 1814.

There was a duel fought close to this town a few weeks ago which unfortunately proved fatal to Mr Heslop who had challenged our attorney, Mr Beynon.

There is little doubt that both would have been killed had not Mr H's pistol gone off, for want of oil or a bad flint, it did not, happily, or the two seconds would have had but a poor chance of saving their lives. They and Mr B immediately absconded but are lately returned to resign themselves at the Assizes.

The young man's brother lives in Jamaica from whence he came four months ago and had been but five weeks at Newcastle Emlyn for the sake of sporting.

When dining with a party at Beynon's house a dispute arose on the subject of shooting which two days later ended fatally.

Mr B's second was his own clerk and Mr H's a son of Mr Abel Walters, Berthgerest [Beddgeraint] who is also an attorney and lives at Newcastle Emlyn with one of his sisters.

Both young men are much blamed having never tried to reconcile the parties, but as Mr Heslop has no friends in England [Britain], I trust they will get off clear, though they deserve twelve month imprisonment.

Mr B is idolised by all the gentlemen near us who will do all to befriend him, consistent with justice, nor could he in their opinion refuse the challenge as a man of honour.

Mr Williams was present at the duel and on his way home over the bridge threw the pistols into the river.

The fatal bullet he has extracted, and it is now in his possession.

### Carmarthenshire Antiquarian Society, Transactions, Vol 17, Page 54.

The letter written by (Mrs) Jennie F. Pridham (not dated) great-granddaughter of Surgeon John Williams and granddaughter of Edward Pridham, many years after the duel, following the publication of the Judges Notes in the Transactions in 1923.

I have read with great interest the account of the Beynon / Heslop duel in 1814, and I think I can venture to say that not many people, if any, now living who can say as I can, of having heard the whole tragic story word for word from my grandmother who at the time was the young wife of Edward Pridham Chemist & Druggist and grandaughter of Dr John Williams. As a little girl I used to pick flowers in the field where the tragedy took place. I remember John Beynon quite well as a tall, very old gentleman. The bullet was in my possession for some years but is now in that of my nephew, Dr A. J. Pridham MC. of Hillfield, Dorset, and I believe is still in the same paper with the names of the seconds written on it.

### Carmarthenshire Antiquarian Society, Transactions., Vol 12, Page 65.

*The letter written by Lettice Jones (later to become Mrs Rogers) to her sister.*

Newcastle, July 15, 1797.

A corps of 500 men had been raised for the defence of the realm called 'The Tivyside Volunteer Corps.' The headquarters of the corps is in Cardigan but the band has been playing in Newcastle Emlyn during a recruitment drive. One of the officers was Captain and Adjutant Dr John Williams, Mr Rogers, a Captain and Mr Lewes of Llysnewydd an Adjutant.

### Carmarthen Journal June 10th 1814. Top Page 1

**To the Unknown Lady** (who addressed a note to the subscriber)

Madam,

Carmarthen, 7th June, 1814.

I cannot express my feelings at the moment. I then publicly acknowledge the great obligation I am under to you for the kind information contained in your note of Monday evening; and although I have no occasion to take advantage of it, still such generous and disinterested conduct to a stranger merits the most grateful acknowledgement: I hope and trust some unforeseen occurrence will give me the power of expressing them personally. And I remain with the highest esteem and respect.

Madam,

Your most obliged and faithful servant.

**THOS. HESLOP**


**Cambrian Index,** Social & Legal 26th March 1825

John Walters of Newcastle Emlyn granted Royal Licence to add the name Phillips after Walters.

**Cardiganshire and its Antiquities,** George Eyre Evans, 1903. Published by the Welsh Gazette

### "Llandyfriog Church"

In the well-ordered burial ground is the grave of Heslop, the unfortunate who was shot by Beynon in the last duel in Cardiganshire, which took place in a glen hard by the church, early one December morning in 1814. Heslop and Beynon had been drinking overnight at the 'Salutation', a tavern then situated at Adpar. Beynon had said things derogatory to the fair fame of the barmaid; to this Heslop objected. High words ensued, and the two men agreed to adjourn to the secluded spot, through which, then as now, meandered a tiny babbling brook. They arranged to stand, one on either side of the stream, and to approach each other backward, then to turn, and instantly fire. Beynon took unfair advantage of his opponent, turned too soon, and shot him in the back. Beynon then left the district; but returned after a while. My father then saw him and conversed with him.

The fatal bullet came into the possession of the surgeon from Newcastle Emlyn who attended the duel – great grandfather of an old school fellow of mine, and in the family this gruesome relic remains. The duel, long since passed into folklore and wayside gossip, created a tremendous sensation at the time; today all we read is the simple inscription on the gravestone, with the exclamation: 'Alas! Poor Heslop.'

# George Eyre Evans, 1857–1939

Was an antiquarian and historian of Welsh Unitarianism. The son of the Rev. David Lewis Evans (1813–1902) minister of the Church of the Saviour at Whitchurch, Salop, he was born at Colyton, County Devon. He became minister of the Church of the Saviour at Whitchurch and also worked hard for the Unitarian Chapel in Aberystwyth. For eighteen years he carried out research for the Royal Commission on Ancient Monuments in Wales and Monmouthshire and was also secretary for the Carmarthenshire Antiquarian Society for thirty three years. He published a number of books in English and also a private magazine, *Antiquarian Notes*, from 1898 until 1905.

## *Walks and Wanderings in County Cardigan*

*E. K. Horsfall-Turner,* **Chapter XVIII, Page 207–208**
**Llandyfriog Church.**

... A glen hard by the church was the scene of the last Cardiganshire duel. On a December morning in 1814, Heslop and Beynon, who had been drinking in the "Salutation" and quarrelled through Beynon's derogatory remarks about the fair name of the barmaid. They agreed to adjourn to the secluded spot and arranged to approach each other backwards and turn then fire. Whether by fair or foul means Beynon shot Heslop in the back and he is buried in the churchyard where his grave reads 'Alas! Poor Heslop'.

## Guide to the Collection of Welsh Bygones, Iorwerth C. Peate, M.A., National Museum of Wales, 1929. Page 132, item 1138.

SPORTING GUN, by John Evans in mahogany case. Said to have been used in a duel at Newcastle Emlyn between two men named Heslop and Beynon. Heslop was a cavalry officer sent to Newcastle Emlyn to quell the Rebecca Riots (c. 1843) and Beynon a solicitor practising at Newcastle Emlyn. Heslop was killed and his body now lies in Llandyfriog churchyard, Card., and over him is a tombstone bearing the inscription: 'Alas! Poor Heslop.' Donor: Sir John Lynn Thomas. (Its accession number is 20.477.)

Description on accession card: percussion cap double barrelled shotgun, with ramrod; engraved John Evans; in felt-lined mahogany case, containing 4 shot flasks (brass), 2 nipple keys, 2 screwdrivers, tin of tallow, tin of percussion caps and powder flask.

With the gun are various letters purporting to tell the story of the duel and the claimed provenance of the gun, a double-barrelled shotgun and not a pistol. One letter states that Heslop was an Army Officer sent to Newcastle Emlyn with his valet to help quell the Rebecca Riots. Heslop had been dead nearly thirty years by then!

It is also suggested that the argument was over the landlady of the Salutation Inn, 'By no means a handsome or fascinating woman.' Much later a Mrs Rees was the landlady of the Salutation Hotel and not of the Old Salutation Inn (Mrs Lodwicke). There is also a copy of a letter written by John Beynon. (Nothing to do with the duel or gun).

The contents of these letters add to the folklore that surrounded the Beynon / Heslop duel of 1814.

(I am grateful to Dylan Jones, Collections Manager at St Fagans Museum, for letting me have copies of the letters. – K.J.)

# *Appendix 7*

## SOME INTERESTING DUELS

A plain, dark stone, dated 1852, marks the final resting place of Frederick Cournet in the village churchyard of Egham a few miles southeast of Windsor. He, a Frenchman, was the last man to die in England in a duel[86]. Ironically his opponent, a man named Barthélémy, was also a Frenchman. The funeral cortège started off from the Barley Mow Inn at Englefield Green with the coffin of Cournet borne on the shoulders of six of his countrymen followed by about a hundred more. The Red Republican Banner tied with black crepe preceded the procession. The French burial ceremony was performed by M. Delescluze in French and an oration was given over the grave. In the evening the French returned as they had arrived, by train from London.

Cournet and Barthélémy met on the 19th October 1852, in a field close to the Barley Mow public house in Englefield Green, between Chertsey and Windsor, Frederick Cournet with his seconds Edmond Allain and Etienne Barronet and Emmanuel Barthélémy with his second, Philippe Eugene Mornet.

They had travelled from London to Windsor by train and then walked to Englefield Green. They had hired the pistols from a shooting gallery in Leicester Square together with twenty two bullets, the same number of percussion caps and a flask of gunpowder. Both the combatants were political refugees and the origin of the duel was political animosity between the parties. Cournet had cast aspersions on the character of Barthélémy and this led to the challenge by Barthélémy. The terms of the duel were thus, that it should begin with pistols, the combatants to stand forty paces apart, advancing ten paces before firing if they chose and having two shots each, misfires not counting; that the choice of position, the choice of pistols and the signal for firing should be determined by tossing up; and if the pistols failed then they would resort to the sword to finish the affair.

Cournet had the choice of pistols and position and his seconds were also to give the signal. He advanced his ten paces, fired, and missed. [This was the first time he had missed hitting his opponent in fourteen duels.] It

86  *The Times*, Monday, October 25, 1852, pg 5

was now Barthélémy's turn to fire and his pistol failed to fire, he put in a fresh cap and tried again with the same result. It was then agreed that he should use Cournet's pistol; this was duly loaded and given to him; he then fired with fatal results.

Dr Hayward of Egham was coming up Priests Hill towards Englefield Green and he passed three foreigners who asked the way to Windsor; a little further on he saw another man coming out of a field. He was approached by this man who asked him to come into the next field where his friend had been injured. He found the deceased lying on the ground with blood flowing from a wound in his side and also found on examination that a ball had passed through his chest from right to left. Dr Hayward then made arrangements for Cournet to be carried to the Barley Mow Inn.

The news of the duel having spread fast a message was sent from Windsor station to Waterloo with a description of the three foreigners. They were duly apprehended at Waterloo. Cournet died a few hours later and the bullet was found in the bed. The pistols were returned to the shooting gallery. It was mentioned that one of them was loaded and when the proprietor tried to fire the pistol it failed, twice; he then unscrewed the breech and found that a piece of cloth was wedged between the powder and the nipple. It would have been impossible to discharge the pistol with the piece of rag in situ.

The prisoners were brought back from London to Windsor and then before the magistrates at Egham. They were then commited for trial.

At the coroners court the jury deliberated for a very short time and gave their verdict, 'Wilful Murder.' The trial[87] took place in March 1853 and the prisoners elected to be tried by a jury composed half of foreigners. They pleaded 'not guilty.' Eventually the jury found them 'Guilty of manslaughter.' The judge passed sentence of a further two months in gaol. Some accounts give Barthélémy as having been hanged for this offence. Barthélémy did in fact die on the scaffold but not until two years later[88] when he was sentenced to death for the murder of George Moore and Charles Collard in Warren Street, London.

---

87   *The Times*, Tuesday March 22, 1853, pg 7
88   *The Times*, Monday, January 8, 1855, pg 6

An earlier duel[89] that took place at Bath also involved foreigners. It was November 1778 when Count Rice and Vicomte du Barri met over a gambling quarrel at Claverton Downs. They, together with their seconds and a surgeon had stayed on the downs all night waiting for the dawn. Rice and du Barri each carried two pistols and a sword.

At dawn the ground was marked out by the seconds and du Barri had the choice of first shot and wounded Rice in the thigh. Count Rice then levelled his pistol and shot du Barri in the breast. Feelings were running very high and they retreated a few yards before rushing at one another and firing again. Both shots missed.

They threw away the pistols and resorted to swords and as they advanced on each other du Barri stopped, grew very pale, fell to the ground and died on the spot. The thigh wound that Rice had received nearly took his life as well and he was dangerously ill for some weeks.

At the inquisition on du Barri's body the jury returned a verdict of 'manslaughter' which caused a few raised eyebrows. Rice was indicted for murder but at his trial the jury found him guilty of manslaughter only and he escaped with a nominal punishment.

One of the most famous duels[90] in United States history took place on July 11, 1804 between Aaron Burr and Alexander Hamilton at Weehawken, New Jersey. Hamilton, the former Treasury secretary died as a result of his wound, former Vice President Burr was indicted for murder but not prosecuted.

Three years earlier Alexander Hamilton's son had been killed in a duel at the same spot using the same set of tricked-out .544 calibre English-made Wogdon pistols. The pistols, which belonged to James Barker Church, Hamilton's brother-in-law, had also been used in a duel between Burr and Church in 1799 (Church may have earlier been forced to flee Britain due to a duel). Legend has it this pair of pistols took the lives of eleven men.

89   *Memoirs of Extraordinary Popular Delusions and the Madness of Crowds,*
     Charles Mackay, 1852
90   *Pistols at Weehawken. The Hamilton / Burr Duel, July 11, 1804,*
     Al Berg & Lauren Sherman, Weehawken Historical Commission, 2004

The last fatal duel[91] in Scotland happened on the 22nd of August 1826. This was fought between David Landale, a linen merchant of Kirkldy and his bank manager George Morgan. As agent for the Bank of Scotland Morgan had refused to accept Landale's bills of exchange. When Landale removed his account from the Bank of Scotland, Morgan spread malicious gossip regarding Landale's finances.

Landale complained to the head office of the Bank of Scotland about Morgan's comments. Morgan found out about the complaint and the next time he met Landale in the street he walloped him with an umbrella.

David Landale was a reluctant duellist but had to maintain his honour and good name so he sent a challenge to Morgan. The arranged duel was to take place at dawn in a field just outside Kirkaldy. Landale who had never fired a shot in anger arrived with his second Mr Millie; Morgan a former military man and used to dealing with guns was accompanied by Lieut. Milne. Also in attendance was a surgeon Dr. Johnson.

In the ensuing duel, Landale fatally wounded Morgan with a shot to the body. The bullet entering on his right side and exiting on the left. Morgan collapsed and died instantly.

At Perth[92] in September 1826 David Landale was tried for the murder of George Morgan. The jury, without retiring, returned a verdict of 'Not guilty.' They, it seemed also agreed, that David Landale was a reluctant duellist and had been provoked.

Perhaps the kind words uttered by his 'Gentry' friends helped:
*Robert Stocks Esq. of Aubden:* I have been well acquainted with Mr Landale for 25 years. I consider him to be a most orderly and correct gentleman, never disposed to quarrel.

*The Provost of Aberdeen:* Had long been acquainted with Mr Landale and found him a man of honour, of mild and gentle manners and most unlikely to provoke quarrels.

*The late Provost of Kirkaldy:* Had known Mr Landale from his infancy. A man of strict honour and a gentleman and he never saw his temper ruffled.

91  *The Times*, Tuesday, August 29 1826, pg 2
92  *The Times*, Wednesday, September 27 1826, pg 3

*Mr Moneypenny of the Custom House, Kirkaldy:* Knew Mr Landale as a gentleman of much mildness and honourable feeling.

This duel is reported as the last between Englishmen on English soil[93]. At the Summer Assizes at Winchester in July 1846, Henry Charles Moorhead Hawkey was indicted for the wilful murder[94] of James Alexander Seton at the Parish of Titchfield on the 20th May 1845 by shooting him with a pistol loaded with powder and a leaden bullet, giving him a mortal wound, of which he died. Mr Seton was late of the 11th Hussars and H. C. M. Hawkey was a Second Lieutenant in the Royal Navy.

Mr Seton and Lieutenant Hawkey were at a soirée held at the King's Rooms on Southsea Beach one evening when it seems that Mr Seton had been paying too much attention to Mrs Hawkey. When the two met in the public rooms later Lieutenant Hawkey called Mr Seton a blackguard and villain and told him that if he would not fight him he would horsewhip him down the Portsmouth High street. He also tried to kick Seton as he left the building.

The consequence was that they met at 5pm at Stoke Bay opposite Ryde on the Gosport shore. Lieutenant Rowles acted as second to Mr Seton and Lieutenant Pym of the Royal Marines was second to Lieutenant Hawkey.

The ground was measured at 15 paces and when the principals were placed the signal was given, Seton fired and missed and Hawkey's pistol did not fire as it had been left at half-cock. Other pistols were supplied to the combatants the signal was again given and both fired. Mr Seton fell and Lieutenant Hawkey immediately left the scene with his second.

Mr Seton received a wound to the right side of his abdomen, the ball passing through and coming out on the left side. An emergency operation was carried out on the 31st May but unfortunately Mr Seton died a few days later from his injuries and peritonitis.

Mr Pym[95] surrendered to the court and was indicted on a charge of killing Mr Seton on March 21st 1846. He was aquitted by the jury.

---

93   *The Times*, Thursday, May 22, 1845, pg 7
94   *The Times*, Friday, July 17, 1846, pg 7
95   *The Times*, Monday, March 9, 1846, pg 7

Mr Hawkey[96] returned from France, where he had been in hiding, and surrendered to the court and was indicted on the same charge as Mr Pym. Mr Hawkey was also found not guilty by the jury and discharged by the judge.

We visited Russia in May 2007 and while on a tour of St. Petersburg, the guide called our attention to a monument we were passing of Alexander Pushkin and told us that he had been killed in a duel. In fact there are several monuments to Pushkin in St. Petersburg including an obelisk where he died in the duel with Georges d'Anthès in 1837.

Pushkin was born in Moscow in June 1799 and was descended from Russian nobility. His great-grandfather was Gannibal, a black general who served under Peter the Great. Pushkin demonstrated an early gift for poetry, publishing his first poem at the age of fourteen.

He moved to St. Petersburg in 1817 to work for the Ministry of Foreign Affairs, he also belonged to a revolutionary underground group. This came to the notice of the authorities and he was exiled, first to Caucasus in 1820 and then banished to his mother's estate near Pskov after being dismissed from government service in 1824. He was pardoned by Tsar Nicholas I, who recognised his popularity and he returned to St. Petersburg.

He proposed to a beautiful woman, Natalie Goncharova, in 1829 when she was only sixteen; she refused but accepted his proposal in 1831 and they were married. She was very popular at court and it is said that Tsar Nicholas gave Pushkin a lowly court title so that he could see more of the lovely Natalie. Pushkin took offence at this. She was invited to every ball at the palace and her frivolous social life led Pushkin into debt. Gossip of an affair between Natalie and Baron Georges d'Anthès was rife and Pushkin received an anonymous note that he had been elected to 'The Serene Order of Cuckolds.'

George d'Anthès had married Natalie's sister but this did not stop Pushkin challenging d'Anthès to a pistol duel in February 1837. They met in the afternoon of the 8th and D'Anthès fired first and Pushkin received the bullet in the stomach. Though badly wounded he managed to fire and D'Anthès received a flesh wound. The bullet that hit Pushkin penetrated the right pelvic bone, continued through the lower abdomen, and crushed

96    *The Times*, Friday, July 17, 1846, pg 7

the right part of the sacral bone. This injury proved fatal and he died two days later probably from peritonitis. D'Anthès[97] recovered from his flesh wound and was found guilty by Court Martial of provoking and killing Pushkin. He was reduced to the ranks and expelled from the Russian nobility. D'Anthès died in 1895.

There were some murmurs of foul play on the part of the Court and that Pushkin had been pushed into this duel. Pushkin was recognised as the greatest Russian poet and the founder of classical Russian poetry and with his death the government feared a political demonstration at his funeral which was moved to a secret location with only close relatives and friends in attendance. His body was spirited away late at night and buried on his mother's estate.

The year 2007 marks the 170th anniversary of Pushkin's death and the State Pushkin Museum in Moscow, itself 50 years old, held an exhibition entitled 'Russian Duel' from February 10th to May 10th 2007. Among the exhibits were a portrait of D'Anthès and the pistol that killed Pushkin. The guns were borrowed for the duel from Ernest de Barante the son of the French Ambassador in 1837.

97  Lord Durham, British Ambassador in St. Petersburg in a dispatch sent to Lord Palmerston, British Foreign Secretary in May 1837 refers to D'Anthès as D'Anthès-Heeckeren, the adopted son of the Dutch Minister

# Appendix 8

DESCRIPTIONS OF NEWCASTLE-IN-EMLYN & ADPAR

J.B. Jnr and W.W. (National Library of Wales Manuscript 23253 C)

Excerpt from:

"A PEDESTRIAN TOUR THREW [sic] WALES IN 1796" (Pages 40 & 41)

By the Rev. James Burgess, Jnr., and William Williams

"Joined the Newcastle Road at Llanrydtridge [Llechryd Bridge] near which are some tin works. [There were tin works at Llechryd].

The walk to Newcastle [Emlyn] is pleasing and the road good... '... and all the air a solemn stillness holds' [Heard a 100 people singing the 104th Psalm]

Newcastle is a miserable village, the accommodation at night as follows. In a cold, dreary, cobwebbed chamber, the thoroughfare to the apartments beyond, stood two beds to receive our weary limbs – the boast of our hostess, who on us entering and asking if she could give us beds exclaimed, 'Oh yes, two excellent ones, I can assure you.'

The bedsteads were made of dirty, rough wood, which had once been covered with paper, but great part of it had torn away. Filthy, stinking, straw mattresses and dirty chequered stuff, nailed on, by way of curtains, ornamented one bed, the other, a piece of paper, seemingly the hanging of a room in the time of Elizabeth. One blanket, two coarse sheets and a nasty rug compounded the furniture of the two beds. An old tottering table and a broken wooden chair contributed to decorate the apartment. The window being broken and patched with paper, the floor full of holes. We were easily seen and we could easily see the people in the kitchen beneath. Behind one of the beds a small cupboard opened just above the bolster, it had no fastening and was filled with all sorts of refuse. The house and apartments were, however, the best the town affords. Anxious to quit the Elysium and hearing we could breakfast a few miles on the road, we started at six without our usual precaution [but found nowhere to eat]."

# Pigot & Co's Trade Directory of 1830

Describes Newcastle-in-Emlyn as a large market hamlet belonging to the Parish of Kennarth in the County of Carmarthen; 234 miles NW from London, 19 NW from Carmarthen and 10 SE from Cardigan.

It is delightfully situated on the river Tivie, which meanders beautifully around the town and its castle. The castle which is seated on a promontory, is the property of the Earl of Cawdor, who derives the additional title of Viscount Emlyn. From this ancient edifice and the surrounding hills some truly beautiful views are obtained.

Newcastle-in-Emlyn is of comparatively modern origin; the ancient town being the old borough of Adpar, in Cardiganshire, formerly of very considerable consequence and known as a Welsh borough long before the Principality was united to England. This ancient Borough was originally a borough by prescription; but a former portreeve, John Lloyd Esq. died in 1741, and the corporate body did not follow the prescription in appointing his successor and therefore forfeited the position.

The town of Newcastle-in-Emlyn is governed by county magistrates and hold their meetings once a fortnight at the "Salutation Inn" (a respectable establishment) where also is held the County Court. The manorial courts of Earl Cawdor, the lord of the manor, are presided over by that nobleman's steward, at the 'Emlyn Arms,' a comfortable inn of considerable repute. The trade is confined to the town and it boasts several respectable and well-furnished shops and their business seems to be thriving. Market day is Friday. Places of worship are a Chapel of Ease under Kennarth and three meeting houses for dissenters.

## An Extract from, "A Topographical Dictionary of Wales" by Samuel Lewis 1833

Describes Adpar as a borough and township in the parish of Llandyvriog, [sic] upper division of the hundred of Troedyraur, county of Cardigan, adjoining the town of Newcastle-Emlyn. This place was formerly one of the contributory boroughs within the county, which were united in returning one member to parliament; but, it forfeited its franchise by misconduct, and was deprived of the privilege by a vote of the House of Commons, in 1742. It has, however, by the bill for amending the representation of the people in England and Wales, been restored to the enjoyment of the elective franchise, and, together with Aberystwith [sic] and Lampeter, shares with

Cardigan in the return of one member. The right of election is vested in every male person of full age occupying, as owner, or as tenant under the same landlord, a house or other premises of the clear yearly value of no less than ten pounds, provided he be capable of registering as the ac directs.

The borough, which is said to have been a borough by prescription, was anciently governed by a portreeve, recorder, and two bailiffs: the burgesses were made on the presentment of a jury, which consisted apparently of the proprietors of burgages, and were accustomed to vote, whether resident or not, for the election of a member: at present there are no burgesses alive. A belief prevails amongst the inhabitants that the charter was destroyed by a fire which occurred within the memory of some now living, in which, there can be no doubt, many of the documents of the borough perished. It comprises within its limits Adpar Hill, the seat of John Beynon, Esq.

## Llandyfriog – Extract from 'A Topographical Dictionary of Wales' by Samuel Lewis 1833.

Describes Llandyfriog as being in the county of Cardigan, one and a half miles east from Newcastle-Emlyn. This parish, which derives its name from the dedication of its church to St. Tyvriog, an eminent British saint who lived towards the close of the sixth century, is pleasantly situated on the northern bank of the river Teivy, and on the turnpike road from Newcastle-Emlyn to Lampeter.

# Appendix 9

## INFORMATION SOURCES

**The National Library of Wales** at Aberystwyth hold records for The Court of Great Sessions of Wales, Crime and Punishment records and the Criminal Register.

**Royal Commission on the Ancient and Historical Monuments of Wales** at Aberystwyth.

**The Ceredigion Archives** at Aberystwyth holds the Quarter Session Records for Cardiganshire.

**The Carmarthenshire Archives** at Carmarthen has microfilmed versions of **The Cambrian, The Welshman,** the **Carmarthen Journal** and **The Times Newspaper.** It also houses the records of the *Carmarthenshire Antiquarian Society* and their publication, **Transactions.**

**The Cambrian.** On 28 January 1804, the first newspaper to be published in Wales, **The Cambrian,** rolled off the press at its premises in Wind Street, Swansea. It carried local and national news, advertisements, notices and social discourse for 126 years, its final weekly issue appearing in March 1930 when it merged with other newspapers to become the new **Herald of Wales.**

**The Cambrian Indexing Project.** The Cambrian Indexing Project http://www.swansea.gov.uk/_info/cambrian/ was established some years ago at Swansea Central Library, with the aim of providing researchers with speedy access to the wealth of information contained within the newspaper's pages.

**The Proceedings of the Old Bailey, London 1674 to 1834,** http://www.oldbaileyonline.org – A fully searchable online edition of texts detailing the lives of non-elite people, containing accounts of over 100,000 criminal trials held at London's central criminal court.

**The Times Digital Archive, 1785 - 1985,** http://infotrac.galegroup.com (Thomson Gale Database). Accessed through ATHENS via the National Library of Wales.

# Appendix 10

*National Library of Wales, Crime and Punishment File No. 4/912/.* *Document No 57.*

*Spring Great Sessions Poster, Wednesday 22nd March 1815,*

*Shire Hall Cardigan. Calendar of Criminal Prisoners for Trial.*

Listed in the Calendar is Evan Davies, late of the Parish of Llandefriog, aged 22 years, committed by William Lewes, Esq. Evan Davies was charged with burglariously and feloniously breaking and entering the premises of Rachel Lodwicke, Elinor Lodwicke and Elizabeth Lodwicke, the Salutation Inn, at Adpar in the Parish of Llandyfriog at eleven o'clock at night on the 23rd October 1814.

He was charged with stealing, one Five Pound Bristol Bill; one Bank of England Note, value One Pound; one Carmarthen Bill, value Two Pounds; with several other Bank Bills and two pieces of the gold coin of this realm, called Guineas, of the value of £2:2 shillings: one piece of the gold coin of this realm, called a Seven Shilling piece, of the value of seven shillings and one silver seal to the value of Three Pounds.

He was sentenced to death by the Judge Serjeant Samuel Heywood, but reprieved, according to the **Cambrian Index** of *8th April 1815.*

# *Appendix 11*

## FURTHER READING

ιe History of Duelling, Millingen J. G. Pub. R. Bentley, London.

ιe Book of Duels, Rush P. Pub. Harrap, 1964.

hat damn'd thing called honour' – duelling in Irish history, ·70–1860, Kelly J. Pub. Cork University Press, 1995.

ιe Last Duel, Landale J. Pub. Canongate Books Ltd., 2005.

ιe Last Duel, Beardsley M. Pub. Barrington Stoke Ltd., March 2007.

stols at Dawn, Hopton R. Pub. Portrait Books, 2007.

Guide to the Records of Great Sessions in Wales, Parry G. Pub. National brary of Wales, 1995.